TECHNOLOGY, PLANNING, AND SELF-RELIANT DEVELOPMENT

TECHNOLOGY, PLANNING, AND SELF-RELIANT DEVELOPMENT

A Latin American View

FRANCISCO R. SAGASTI

 PRAEGER PUBLISHERS
Praeger Special Studies

New York • London • Sydney • Toronto

Library of Congress Cataloging in Publication Data

Sagasti, Francisco R
   Technology, planning, and self-reliant development.

   Includes bibliographical references.
   1. Underdeveloped areas--Technology. I. Title.
T49.5.S2313   309.2'22'091724   78-26010
ISBN 0-03-047221-0

PRAEGER PUBLISHERS
PRAEGER SPECIAL STUDIES
383 Madison Avenue, New York, N.Y. 10017, U.S.A.

Published in the United States of America in 1979
by Praeger Publishers,
A Division of Holt, Rinehart and Winston, CBS, Inc.

9   038   987654321

For:

Geoffrey Oldham and Máximo Halty (the "Godfathers"),
and to my friends and colleagues of the Science and
Technology Policy Instruments (STPI) Project.

NAM ET IPSA SCIENTIA POTESTAS EST

Francis Bacon

PREFACE

The thinking on science, technology, and development that prevailed during the 1960s presented a rather optimistic and simplistic view of the complex interrelations among modern science, science-based technology, and the processes of development and underdevelopment. The following statement is representative of the ideas of that period:

> It is true that modern science and technology have widened the gap between the rich and the poor countries, but that is because the advanced countries have been in a better position to use them. Enlisted more widely in the service of the developing countries, science and technology can help them reduce that gap; in particular, they provide short cuts to the goals of development and can spare the new countries some of the slow process of trial and error that the advanced countries had to pass through. The developing countries can take advantage of the rate of technological change since the Second World War which has been much faster than ever in history.*

Recently this view has been questioned as a result of new ideas in development theory, of empirical evidence about the impact of modern science and technology on the Third World, and of the frustrating experience of two decades of science and technology policy making in underdeveloped countries.

New theories have challenged the linear and sequential conception of development associated with the idea of closing the gap between rich and poor countries, and have emphasized the structural interdependencies between the processes of development and underdevelopment. Science and technology have been found to be at the root of an unequal international division of labor between advanced and underdeveloped countries, and instead of providing short

---

*United Nations, <u>Science and Technology for Development: World of Opportunity</u> (New York: United Nations, 1963), vol. 1, p. 185. Report of the United Nations Conference on the Application of Science and Technology for the Benefit of the Less Developed Areas.

cuts to development, they have been contributing to widening the differences between them. The accelerated pace of technological change after World War II has provided the industrialized nations with new means for increasing their domination over the Third World, and there is no apparent way in which the less developed countries can take advantage of the new technological advances, particularly if autonomy and self-reliance are postulated as desired characteristics of the development process.

The 1970s are witnessing a transition in our understanding of the potential contribution of science and technology (S and T) to the development of the poor nations, and of the conditions under which this contribution can be made effective. The present book is a product of this decade of transition. It has been written from a Latin American perspective on the basis of conceptual studies, of empirical observations, and of reflections resulting from the author's experience as researcher, research coordinator, and policy maker. The book focuses on industrial technology and on policies for developing an autonomous scientific and technological capacity. Even though they are based mainly on the Latin American experience, discussions in Africa, Asia, and the Middle East have shown that the main issues identified here are relevant to a variety of contexts of underdevelopment.

The central theme developed throughout the book is the idea that science and technology are closely interconnected with the processes of development and underdevelopment. The generation and control of modern science-based technology will increasingly become the principal means through which a few highly industrialized countries will exert domination over the Third World, particularly as the latter gathers new strength and begins to control the means through which the industrialized countries exerted their domination in the past, such as the direct exploitation of natural resources, the establishment and management of productive facilities, and the provision of finance. Each chapter of the volume deals with some aspect of the way in which the underdeveloped countries can organize themselves to develop their own S and T capabilities, and to devise appropriate responses to the pressures of the highly industrialized countries. Thus Chapter 1 starts from a conceptualization of underdevelopment, examines its relation to science and technology, and points out three conditions that must be met to alter the existing state of affairs: the redistribution of the international scientific and technological effort; the development of indigenous scientific and technological capabilities in Third World countries; and the full incorporation of technological considerations in the development planning process.

A second common theme behind these essays is the need for purposeful state intervention to bring about S and T development. This implies a rejection of the concept that market forces on their own will lead to the development of scientific and technological capabilities in the less developed countries, and introduces the subject of S and T planning. The organization of state intervention requires a consciousness of the importance of S and T capabilities for self-reliant development; a strong political commitment to the development of indigenous science and technology; and the use of a variety of government policy instruments, including those aimed explicitly at the development of science and technology, and those affecting other development policies that have significant technological implications. These ideas and the scope for science and technology planning in underdeveloped countries are treated in Chapters 2 and 3. Chapter 2 examines the difficulties involved in the S and T planning process, while Chapter 3 suggests a normative framework for the organization of state intervention in S and T development.

A third main theme of the book is that the diversity of conditions of underdevelopment preclude the design of universal models for S and T development that can be strictly applied to all situations. What may be legitimately done is to postulate general principles, abstracted from experience and reflection, that should be reinterpreted in each specific context of underdevelopment. In the process of abstracting and reinterpreting general principles and guidelines, policy-oriented research plays a most significant role. In this regard, Chapter 4 presents the conceptual framework that was used in the research of the Science and Technology Policy Instruments (STPI) project,* while Chapter 5 proposes some general principles and guidelines that have been abstracted from technology policy research and from the experience of the Latin American countries.

The importance of S and T collaboration among less developed countries is another recurrent theme of the book. It is postulated as one of the necessary conditions for the Third World in facing the S and T pressures exerted by the highly industrialized countries (Chapter 1). The efforts of the Andean Pact countries to design a common technology policy are examined in Chapter 6. At a more

---

*See Francisco Sagasti, <u>Science and Technology for Development</u> (Ottawa: International Development Research Centre, IDRC), 1978). Main Comparative Report of the Science and Technology Policy Instruments (STPI) Project.

general level, Chapter 9 examines the issue of technological co-operation among less developed countries, putting it in the broader context of collective self-reliance, and suggesting criteria for the organization of collaborative efforts in science and technology.

The problem of institutional development for S and T is also examined throughout the book. In this regard, two institutions that have played a significant role in the less developed countries are the industrial research institutes and the universities. Chapter 7 examines the case of the Industrial Technology Institute in Peru (ITINTEC—Instituto de Investigación Tecnológica Industrial ye de Normas Técnicas) and the mechanisms that were devised for linking it with the productive sector and for augmenting the flow of financial resources to industrial technology research. Chapter 8 deals with the institutional infrastructure for S and T, focusing on the universities, whose role in technological development has been the subject of heated debate in Latin America.

The last chapter presents a reinterpretation of the processes of development and underdevelopment in S and T terms. It offers a historical perspective of the interactions between Western science, science-based technology, and the traditional technological base, both in the developed and underdeveloped countries, examining the conditions that may lead to the endogenization of the scientific and technological revolution. This closing chapter represents an attempt to bring together the various strands of thought that are behind the studies contained in the book.

ACKNOWLEDGMENTS

There are many colleagues I should thank for their contribution and assistance in the preparation of this book. The age of researchers who work in isolation passed a long time ago, and perhaps never existed in a field so new as science and technology policy. In particular I would like to thank Enrique Felices, a long-time friend and colleague; Máximo Halty and Alejandro Moya, who helped me to start working in this field; Russell Ackoff, Eric Trist, and Ignacy Sachs, from whom I learned so much; Mauricio Guerrero and Pedro León Diaz, colleagues during my stay at the Secretariat of the Andean Pact; and Isaías Flit and Gustavo Flores, with whom I worked in the design and establishment of the Peruvian Industrial Technology Institute. Furthermore, I also benefited from many discussions with Jorge Sabato, Amílcar Herrera, Marcel Roche, Miguel Wionczek, Henrique Rattner, Enrique Oteiza, Carlos Martínez Vidal, and Mario Kamenetzky, who have done so much to develop the Latin American school of thought in science and technology policy.

I owe special gratitude to Geoffrey Oldham, who has been a constant source of support and encouragement. He was instrumental in my continuing to work in this field as coordinator of the Science and Technology Policy Instruments project. I also owe a great deal to my coworkers in that project, particularly to Alejandro Nadal, Jose Tavares, KunMo Chung, Fabio Erber, Fernando Chaparro, Eduardo Amadeo, Anil Malhotra, Alberto Araoz, Phactuel Rego, Sergio Barrio, Onelia Cardettini, and Carlos Contreras, with whom I interacted closely for more than three years. Last, but not least, I want to thank Blanca Stella Herrera for her careful and cheerful typing and retyping of the long and messy manuscript.

CONTENTS

LIST OF TABLES

LIST OF FIGURES

TECHNOLOGY, PLANNING, AND SELF-RELIANT DEVELOPMENT

1

Underdevelopment, Science, and Technology

INTRODUCTION

This chapter examines the interrelations between underdevelopment, science, and technology from the viewpoint of the underdeveloped countries. The central thesis is that science and technology have been closely associated with the emergence of underdevelopment, and that to a certain extent they are contributing to its maintenance and persistence. In order to modify this situation, major structural changes are required both in the way scientific and technological activities are organized within the less developed countries, and in the international structure of the world scientific and technological effort. These changes will not come automatically. They must be pressed and initiated by the developing countries themselves.

Underdevelopment is a phenomenon in its own right. It cannot be adequately studied and interpreted as a stage in a sequential development process, or as an interval in a development continuum along which all countries can be placed, and through which all must proceed in order to become developed. As Celso Furtado[1] and Oswaldo Sunkel and Pedro Paz[2] have shown, underdevelopment, particularly in Latin America, is a consequence of the historical process of industrialization in Europe and later in North America. Development and underdevelopment are thus two facets of the same process of expansion of Western capitalism that began in the nineteenth century. This process involved the creation and spread of

Used with permission from a paper first published in <u>Science Studies</u> 3, no. 1 (1973): 47-59. Permission granted by Sage Publications, Ltd., London.

modern technology and the establishment of an international division of labor with a few more advanced countries generating modern technology and producing manufactured goods, and a large number of backward countries supplying raw materials, cheap labor, and markets. Underdevelopment and development evolved simultaneously; they were and are functionally related and they also interact with and condition each other. These two phenomena must, therefore, be understood as interdependent parts of a single system. The key factor differentiating these structures is that the developed, by virtue of its endogenous capacity for growth--based on technical progress and capital accumulation--became dominant, and the underdeveloped, because of its incapacity for growth, became passive, dependent, and dominated.

Characteristics of Underdeveloped Countries

As a first approximation it is possible to characterize an underdeveloped country as one that is dominated, disarticulated, and incapable of providing an adequate standard of living for the majority of its population.[3] Domination implies that the underdeveloped country does not have a capacity for autonomous decision making, and that it exercises little control over its own destiny. External factors, beyond the control of the underdeveloped country, are the main determinants of its economic, social, and even political decisions.

Domination is formally defined as a bilateral and asymmetric relationship, irreversible in the short and medium terms, so characterized because a change in the dominant unit invariably results in a change in the dominated unit, whereas a similar change in the latter has little or no effect on the former.[4] Domination may thus be considered an extreme form of dependence. The primary form of domination of underdeveloped countries by developed ones is economic, although this is closely related to cultural and technical domination, with one of them leading to or implying the others.

Developed countries have been continuously shifting their modes of domination over underdeveloped ones in response to changing conditions and to pressures from them. From the control of raw materials extracted from the underdeveloped countries and of the manufactured goods they supplied, developed countries gained control of a significant share of the productive activities and later shifted to the control of financing, moving at present to control of the technology required in productive and social activities. This control is acquired through direct investment, through licensing agreements, through the provision of equipment and machinery, through the sale of patents, and through management contracts and technical assistance agreements. The primary vehicle through which these various forms of domination are exerted is the transnational corporation.

Disarticulation means that the underdeveloped country does not constitute a homogeneous unit from the cultural, social, and economic points of view. It is a highly stratified society with little or no interaction among the various strata and with almost no mobility between them. There is in particular a high-income stratum which is more closely related to the developed countries, particularly to the large cosmopolitan urban centers, than to other strata within the underdeveloped country. This high-income social group has been present from the beginning of the process of underdevelopment, although its composition has changed with time. Through a process of alienation it has become part of a global consumist elite, which adopts foreign consumption habits and is fully identified with the values and life styles prevailing in the dominant countries. This social group exerts a strong pressure toward an imitative diversification of the consumer goods basket and the dispersion of productive activities, forcing the importation of the technologies required to sustain a pattern of consumption induced from abroad.

As a result of the social disarticulation and of the separation existing among the diverse social strata, improvements in socioeconomic conditions generally affect only some segments of the population (professionals, landowners, unionized workers), leaving the other segments or compartments (peasants, unskilled workers) comparatively unchanged.

The third characteristic, the incapacity to provide an adequate standard of living for the majority of the population, is the most striking of the three. The majority of the world population, which is concentrated in the underdeveloped countries of the Third World, has a very low and often deteriorating standard of living, and the traditional aid and trade measures have proven insufficient to improve social conditions. For example, the Inter-American Development Bank in its periodic reports on socioeconomic progress repeatedly points out deficiencies in practically all aspects of living conditions in most countries in Latin America. Shortages in housing, high infant mortality, low life expectancy, malnutrition, lack of educational opportunities, and marked inequalities in income distribution appear to be normal for the majority of Latin Americans. Furthermore, these characteristics of underdevelopment show no signs of being overcome.

These three characteristics of the process of underdevelopment are intimately related to the problem of capital accumulation, which determines the capacity for endogenous economic growth. An economy can grow in a sustained way and without resorting to permanent transfers from abroad only if it generates an economic surplus which, after providing for the needs of the labor force, will be capable of feeding into the expansion of the productive system in such a way that it may, in turn, continue to satisfy the future needs of the population and improve their standard of living without resorting to artificial controls.

Oscar Lange defines an underdeveloped economy as "that in which the available stock of capital goods is not sufficient to employ all the labor force using modern production techniques."[5] From this perspective the options are (a) to employ a larger share of the labor force with backward techniques which, due to their low productivity, do not generate the sufficient economic surplus to ensure an acceptable level of per capita income and a viable process of accumulation; or (b) to adopt advanced or modern techniques with high productivity, which would cause unemployment for a large part of the labor force, because the capital available does not permit the employment of all the labor force with the use of modern capital-intensive techniques. The immobilization of a good part of the labor force impedes the generation of a surplus that would be sufficient to cover the cost of an adequate standard of living for all the population, while at the same time feeding into a continuous and sustained process of capital accumulation.

These statements contain an implicit temporal dimension, for they can be formulated as a choice between privileging, on the one hand, the use of capital-intensive techniques that could generate a larger surplus that in the future might be devoted (through the expansion of the modern sector of the economy) to the absorption of the marginated labor force; and on the other hand, giving more emphasis to the utilization of relatively backward techniques, which--because they incorporate a larger share of the labor force into productive activities--would increase present consumption at the expense of generating surplus to expand the modern sector in the future.

The two choices put forward by Lange coexist separately in the less developed countries between and within the different productive branches. Because the second option--use of high productivity techniques--is characteristic of the modern branches and productive units of industry, mining, and agriculture, and because these are usually linked directly to the interests of the dominating countries, the surplus they generate is mostly transferred abroad, limiting further the possibility of achieving a viable accumulation process. At the same time, that part of the surplus that remains within the country is appropriated by the stratum of the population involved in modern productive activities, those who have relatively high incomes and who adopt foreign consumption patterns. Because their group privileges are associated with the maintenance of the existing order, they show little interest in channeling the surplus they appropriate toward a capital-accumulation process that would lead to sustained economic growth and to substantial socioeconomic transformations, preferring to use their portion of the surplus for consumption of a more luxurious sort.

The two options put forward by Lange are extreme cases and do not exhaust the range of technological possibilities. It is feasible to identify and design combined production techniques that would incorporate traditional and modern components in an integrated way, so as to use more effectively the available factors of production, thus increasing productivity and obtaining an economic surplus adequate for local conditions. This option has not been systematically explored and developed, because it did not respond to the interests which oriented technical progress during the last two centuries. [6] (For an elaboration of this theme see Chapter 10.)

But even if the productive system could generate a surplus on which to base a viable capital-accumulation process, in order to achieve endogenous economic growth it would be necessary to count on the capacity to transform this surplus into reproducible capital goods with the appropriate technical characteristics. In turn, this capacity is determined by the scientific and technological level of the country, by the existence of a capital goods industry, and by the effective combination of both. Without this capacity, the accumulated surplus must be used to purchase capital goods in the industrialized countries, which would lead once again to new forms of dependency.

Taking into consideration these issues, development can be defined as a dynamic process of structural change characterized by three factors: sustained economic growth linked to a viable capital-accumulation process; scientific and technological progress which would ensure the possibility of transforming the surplus into capital goods with the adequate technical characteristics; and social propagation of the effects of economic growth and technical progress to all sectors of the population.

The first factor, economic growth, has traditionally been considered synonymous with development. Although a necessary condition, it is not sufficient by itself, because economic growth without technological progress and the propagation of their effects does not overcome the conditions of domination and disarticulation that characterize underdevelopment.

The second factor, scientific and technological progress, refers to the autonomous capacity of a country to generate, disseminate, and utilize technological knowledge in its productive and social processes. This capacity would permit designing productive techniques adequate for local conditions, and would assist industry in the transformation of economic surplus into capital goods without resorting to a relationship of technological dependence. However, acquiring autonomy in technological matters does not necessarily imply the total rejection of imported technology; rather, it requires the ability to select, evaluate, negotiate, absorb, and modify foreign know-how, adapting it to local conditions and even reexporting it after further development.

The third and last factor refers to the distribution of the fruits of economic growth and of technical progress throughout the population. This is equivalent to eliminating the disarticulation that characterizes underdeveloped countries, distributing the benefits associated with the development process to the various regions of the country and to all sectors of society, so as to raise the living conditions of all to an acceptable level.

To these factors that characterize a development process, it is necessary to add one condition: the development process must be self-reliant. Self-reliance is to be understood for each underdeveloped country on its own level, as the will to build up and use a capacity for autonomous decision making and implementation on all aspects of the development process. In this sense it stands against all forms of dependence, and the extent to which this condition will be realized in practice will depend on the room for maneuver that a particular underdeveloped country has. Self-reliance has been further characterized in the following terms by Ashok Parthasarathi:

> The approach to self-reliance is reflected internationally as opposition to all forms of dependence; it calls for changing the mode of insertion of the developing countries in the international political, economic and cultural system; if the predicament of "helplessness" in which many developing countries find themselves is to be avoided, they have to recapture and internalize the centers of decision making on their destiny; this may call, in certain cases, for developing countries to temporarily detach themselves from the present world system and then recouple with that system on a new basis at a later date. What would be the most appropriate way of doing this has to be decided by each country in the context of its own predicament and needs. [7]

On the basis of these observations it is possible to identify some prerequisites for initiating and sustaining a self-reliant development process. First, it is necessary to develop the capacity for autonomous decision making to the fullest possible extent permitted by the particular context and conditions of a given underdeveloped country. Second, it is necessary to avoid the waste of the economic surplus generated in the country (mainly by the modern sector of the economy). This implies eliminating or reducing the relationships of dependence that transfer the surplus to the industrialized countries (through unfavorable terms of trade and through open and hidden financial flows), and also modifying the patterns of consumption induced from abroad, so that the surplus remaining in the country will be available for transformation into savings and investment. Third, it is necessary to increase the magnitude of the surplus, which requires counting on an indigenous scientific and technological capacity to develop production techniques appropriate to local conditions. During the first stage, this capacity would help in adopting the most suitable technology from the industrialized nations. These measures do not in any way cover all the transformations that are necessary to achieve a self-reliant development process. However, they give an idea of the key role that science and technology play in overcoming underdevelopment.

INTERRELATIONSHIPS OF SCIENCE, TECHNOLOGY, AND UNDERDEVELOPMENT

In the past three decades, technology has become increasingly important as a factor in the relations between developed countries, as well as in the relations between developed and underdeveloped countries. Technological progress has been credited with contributing more than any other factor to the economic growth of developed countries, both East and West, and until very recently resources allocated to research and development in advanced countries have been growing at an exponential rate. In addition, the technological content of manufactured goods has become a major determinant of the patterns of trade between developed countries, and also between developed and underdeveloped countries. [8]

Most underdeveloped countries, waging a losing battle with the deterioration of the terms of trade, have seen the steady increase of the technological content of their imports. At the same time they have realized that it is becoming more and more difficult to manufacture goods for export in competition with firms and countries with vastly superior scientific and technological capabilities.

For the underdeveloped countries that followed the route of import substitution to begin their industrialization (Latin American countries, for example), the industrialization process--which began with the substitution of consumer products and then moved on to technologically more complex goods--demonstrated that each new wave of import substitution generated a demand for increasingly more complex and advanced technologies and equipment. These were usually provided by the industrialized nations, because the incipient industrial, scientific, and technological infrastructure of the underdeveloped countries had no capacity to provide either the know-how or the capital goods required in productive activities. The situation is not too different in the countries that switched to an export-oriented industrialization strategy in the late 1960s, for their markets are located mostly in the United States, Japan, and Western Europe, which implies that productive techniques must be imported for the manufacture of export goods to satisfy the consumption habits, tastes, and quality requirements of the markets in industrialized nations.

Therefore, more frequently than not, efforts to industrialize have led to increased technological dependence. Furthermore, rapid advances in science and technology in the industrialized nations (which make obsolete the existing stock of scientific and technological knowledge in less developed countries), the acute backwardness in science and technology of the less developed world, and the increasing importance of (and need for) modern science-based technologies in key productive and social activities are making technological domination the major form of domination of underdeveloped countries by developed ones in the second half of the twentieth century.

Most of the technology available in the world today has been created in the developed countries. It has been estimated by the Sussex Group that in 1964 fully 98 percent of the world's expenditures on research and development were made by developed countries. [9] Moreover, the 2 percent spent by the underdeveloped countries was often misused, allocated to research tasks of little consequence for development and to research centers with lower productivity than the average in developed countries. More recent estimates put these figures at 96 percent and 4 percent, respectively, in 1973, which shows that little has changed in one decade. [10]

The research and development activity in developed countries is concentrated in a few large corporations or government-backed organizations, as shown by a variety of studies. [11] These conditions have led to the formation of Research and Development (R & D) oligopolies in almost every branch of economic activity, and particularly in those where science-based technologies occupy a prominent position. This concentrates the power to exert technological domination in a rather limited number of firms in the industrialized countries, which have virtual monopolies over the supply of technology, particularly in relation to underdeveloped countries. Moreover, the absolute level of the R & D effort in developed countries is several orders of magnitude larger than that of the underdeveloped

countries, and the existence of a cumulative scientific and technological tradition in the developed countries makes it difficult for an
underdeveloped country, or even a group of them, to reach the
levels of achievement attained by the developed ones in almost every
area of science and technology. As a consequence, much of the existing stock of scientific and technological knowledge is suited to the
needs and conditions prevailing in developed countries, which have
little in common with those of the underdeveloped ones. (Technologies that require large amounts of capital, large-scale production,
and highly skilled labor provide one example.) Needless to say,
these hardly correspond to the situations prevailing in underdeveloped countries.

Furthermore, current trends in scientific and technological
research will intensify this divergence.[12] Among the characteristic
trends in the development of new technology, it is possible to identify
a shift toward more automated plant equipment using limited but
highly skilled labor, and toward increases in the economic scale of
productive units. There is also a trend toward the development of
new synthetic materials, which has potentially dangerous implications for underdeveloped countries because they depend largely on
the export of raw materials and primary commodities for their foreign exchange.

Underdeveloped countries thus face a lack of suitable technological alternatives. Often they are faced with the dilemma of choosing between increasing industrial output by using modern, generally
capital-intensive techniques, or foregoing opportunities for increasing output but maintaining relatively higher levels of employment by
using obsolete techniques. The lack of viable and efficient technological alternatives, together with the underdeveloped countries' low
scientific and technological capacities, pose a difficult challenge,
particularly in view of the explosive conditions of population growth,
unemployment, and underemployment. In some cases the lack of
viable alternatives and the ignorance of the buyer of technology in
underdeveloped countries has led to the waste of scarce resources,
particularly capital. Heavy investments have too often been made
in plants with capacities vastly exceeding the size of the market. In
some cases governments in underdeveloped countries have encouraged the proliferation of oversize plants for the sake of achieving
competition (in accordance with conventional economic wisdom),
with the net result of higher costs, inefficiency, and dilapidation of
resources.

The capacity for creating technology, or even absorbing imported technology, is not present in most underdeveloped countries.
As a result of the passive character of their economic growth, their
demands for technology have usually been satisfied from abroad,

through the import of equipment and through technical assistance by foreign technicians. Because foreign technology has been readily accessible, little pressure has been exerted on the local scientific community to provide viable technological alternatives, particularly in the manufacturing industries. Industrialization policies, fostering technological dependence, have often accentuated the cleavage between the local scientific community and the technological needs of the country. In consequence underdeveloped countries find themselves incapable of creating and satisfying their technological needs, and even incapable of selecting and absorbing the most suitable imported technology from the limited range available. Furthermore, as the studies carried out by Constantine Vaitsos,[13] and Gastón Oxman and Francisco Sagasti[14] show, foreign technologies are more often than not acquired under very unfavorable conditions, which include high implicit and explicit costs, and restrictions on their use.

Because the productive sectors of the economy exert little pressure on the local scientific and technological communities, scientists and researchers orient themselves toward the international scientific community, choosing research topics in fashion, seeking to contribute to the advancement of science as an international undertaking, and disregarding the specific research needs of their countries. As long as these needs are ignored by the local scientific communities, they can retain their identity only by orienting themselves outwards. Thus one finds local scientific communities of many underdeveloped countries alienated from their own environment and zealously defending freedom of research and the values of universal science, to the detriment of their potential contribution to the development of their own countries. The well-known phenomenon of "brain-drain" is an extreme manifestation of this alienation.

The international scientific community, erring by omission rather than deliberately, has contributed to increase this alienation. Not enough attention has been given by scientists to the scientific and technological problems particular to underdeveloped countries. Ignacy Sachs[15] postulates that the Europocentric character of modern Western science has had a retarding effect on the scientific efforts of underdeveloped countries. Estimates by the Sussex Group[16] indicate that less than 1 percent of the total research effort in developed countries, to which the international scientific community is primarily related, is directly relevant to the problems of underdevelopment, although the amount may be of the same order of magnitude as the expenditures by underdeveloped countries themselves. Prestige is conferred on researchers who work on exotic and sophisticated advanced topics, choice of which is often dictated by scientific fashion or novelty. Most of these have nothing to do with the more pedestrian scientific and technical problems faced by underdeveloped countries.

The insistence on the international and universal character of the scientific enterprise, the rejection of the imposition of any type of control in the selection of research topics and areas, and the emphasis on the objectivity of science and its quest for truth have all been proposed as characteristics of what Michael Polanyi[17] has called the "Republic of Science." These, advocated as indispensable conditions for pursuing science, have also had some effect on the behavior of the scientific community in underdeveloped countries. Any attempt to reorientate the local scientific effort, gearing it to the needs of the country, is arduously fought by scientists, who see it as infringing on their rights, jeopardizing the integrity of their undertaking, and tampering with the freedom of research.

Little attention is paid by the advocates of unrestricted scientific freedom to the implicit guidance of the scientific enterprise in developed countries through the manipulation of resources available for research. The fact that investments in research soared after World War II, primarily in defense, atomic energy, and space, is not taken into account. Scientists, professionals, and technicians, preoccupied with the freedom to choose their own individual research topics, are not generally aware of the fact that the broad directions of scientific progress have been primarily influenced by political, economic, and social considerations.

It must be emphasized that scientists in underdeveloped countries have acted in a rational way in the process of becoming alienated. Given the lack of effective demand for their services in their countries and the structure of the international scientific community, they could not help, if they were willing to remain scientists, but choose research topics sanctioned by the international scientific community, for which resources have been often more freely available. This is but another instance of the divorce between individual and collective rationality in underdeveloped countries.

The preceding paragraphs have dwelt on the aspects of the present organization of scientific and technological activities that do not appear to contribute to socioeconomic development in underdeveloped countries. This was done primarily because the literature on this subject has emphasized the positive contributions of science and technology to development. This optimistic view must be tempered by the realization that the science and technology of developed nations are not, in the main, the kind required in underdeveloped countries; the part that is required is not usually available under favorable conditions; and if it is, there is often a lack of competence to use it.

This is not to deny that science and technology can and will contribute to development. There are many examples showing that scientific findings, and the technologies derived from them, can be of great assistance in alleviating some of the most extreme manifestations of underdevelopment, particularly in the health field. Only latter-day Luddites would refuse to recognize their potential contribution. Therefore, in summing up it could be said that science and technology have the potential to contribute, perhaps more than any other single factor, to overcoming the conditions of underdevelopment. However, the present structures of scientific and technological activities in both developed and underdeveloped countries are such that this potential is not being fully realized. Rather, they appear to reinforce, at least partially, the conditions of underdevelopment.

EFFECTUATING THE POTENTIAL CONTRIBUTION OF SCIENCE AND TECHNOLOGY TO DEVELOPMENT

From the preceding analysis it follows that if science and technology are to contribute to the development of the Third World, there must be a major transformation in the structure of the world scientific and technological effort. The necessary changes, which require a firm commitment by both developed and underdeveloped countries, can be grouped into three categories: (1) modifications in the international division of labor and the orientation of scientific and technological activities at the world level; (2) generation of local scientific and technological capabilities in underdeveloped countries; and (3) full incorporation of science and technology within the scope of development planning efforts.

Redistribution of International Scientific and Technological Effort

The first group of changes would include measures to ensure that a larger portion of world expenditures in research and development is allocated to projects relevant to underdevelopment. The Sussex Group[18] and the United Nations[19] have suggested targets for the percentage of research and development expenditures by developed countries that should be devoted to the problems of underdeveloped countries (figures around 1-2 percent have been mentioned), and for the percentage of total aid from developed to underdeveloped countries that should be oriented toward the generation of local scientific and technological capabilities.* These proposals involve primarily bilateral forms of science and technology aid. On their own they are not likely to have a major effect on the nature and distribution of world expenditures on science and technology. At best they would succeed in improving research and development in specific fields for some underdeveloped countries. At worst they would make the development of local scientific and technological capabilities more dependent on specific foreign sources.

Another proposal along this line seeks to establish multilateral research and development funds at the world and/or regional levels. These funds would operate with their own independent and stable financial sources, which could be provided by special taxes or duties on activities that are realized at the world level. (For example, Sachs in a personal communication has suggested that programs to control sea pollution be financed with taxes levied on ships operating in international waters.) Voluntary contributions made by underdeveloped countries and matched by developed countries could provide additional funds, but could not replace an independent and stable source of money. However, the availability of funds does not per se constitute a guarantee that the science and technology financed with them will have an impact on the development of the Third World. If these funds were administered by scientists from underdeveloped countries alienated from their own environment, and/or if scientists from developed countries were not aware of the complex interrelations between science, technology, and underdevelopment, the distortions found at present in the world scientific and technological effort would probably be reinforced.

Changes at the international level should also include increased cooperation between underdeveloped countries in matters related to science and technology. Eventually, more intensive collaboration may pave the road for effective scientific and technological integration (see Chapter 9). However, experience has shown that cooperation agreements are relatively easy to reach when issues of a purely scientific nature are involved, but when cooperation or integration programs involve research activities that may have direct economic application--which could benefit a particular country or even a particular enterprise--agreement is much more difficult to obtain. In consequence, scientific and technological integration

---

*At present it appears that Canada, through its International Development Research Center, is effectively moving in the direction of making science and technology a significant component of its aid program.

among underdeveloped countries is likely to be achieved only in conjunction with economic and political integration.

There is also a need for establishing a pressure group that would act on the international scientific community, motivating scientists to become involved in projects of potential or direct benefit to underdeveloped countries. In the face of increased East-West dialogue (and maybe even agreement on nuclear matters) this could be a task for the Pugwash movement. A new generation of scientists-activists who would take the banner of science and technology for the development of the Third World could inject a new sense of purpose into Pugwash. Failing this, it would be necessary to organize a new pressure group, perhaps within the framework of institutions such as the United Nations Conference on Trade and Development (UNCTAD) Group of 77 and the International Council of Scientific Unions, to press these issues before the international scientific community.

The list of possible actions at the international level could be expanded to include the introduction of a technological dimension in the evaluation of projects financed by international development banks or agencies, the establishment of mechanisms to award prestige to scientists working on problems related to development (a Nobel prize has been one suggestion), and the introduction of a development-merit criterion for evaluating proposed research projects (following Weinberg's approach to scientific choice).[20]

Development of Scientific and Technological
Capabilities in Third World Countries

The second group of changes requires action at the national level. In consequence these changes must be tailored to the particularities of a given national situation. Underdeveloped countries are not a homogeneous lot and specific proposals to improve scientific and technological capabilities must take into account differences in size, resources, levels of modernization, cultural patterns, and many other factors. Nevertheless, it is possible to identify some actions that are necessary for the development of a local capacity for science and technology (see Chapter 3).

First, it is necessary that long-term objectives be clearly formulated, defining the style of science and technology that the country is seeking to develop, and its relation to the overall economic and social development strategy.

Second, the interactions between science and technology and the economic, educational, political, and cultural environment of the country must be considered. The environment affects both the demand for knowledge generated by scientific and technological activities and the possibilities for producing it locally. In particular, the characteristics of the economic system and of many government economic policies contain an array of implicit science policies-- which are perhaps more important than explicit policies, and which frequently run against the objectives of scientific and technological development. For example, the implicit science policy contained in the import-substituting industrialization of many Latin American countries has often reinforced technological dependence.[21] (For a discussion of these concepts, see Chapter 4.) Identifying these contradictions and exposing these conflicts is of primary importance for scientific and technological development. As long as negative implicit policies remain hidden, it will be impossible to remove the obstacles that prevent scientific and technological development.

The development of a local institutional infrastructure for science and technology is a third aspect that must be covered. Institutions are the means through which resources are channeled to scientific and technological activities. A wide and well-organized base of institutions constitutes a necessary condition for attaining an acceptable level of scientific and technological development.

Underdeveloped countries cannot expect to excel in all fields of science and technology. Therefore, a fourth aspect to consider is the need for a strategy of specialization to be followed by the generation of a local capacity for science and technology. This implies a choice of domains in which the underdeveloped country would become an advanced center of knowledge to which resources would be allocated with priority. In other fields or domains technology could be imported, although it would be necessary to exert control on these imports to avoid the negative effects that often accompany them. However, this strategy does not imply abandoning the support that fundamental science is required to provide--for example, a base of scientific activity and qualified manpower for science and technology. A balance must be achieved between the concentration of resources in some domains and the general support that fundamental science must receive.

The last aspect to consider refers to the availability of resources for science and technology. Human, financial, and physical resources must be provided beyond the minimum critical mass, particularly in the domains chosen by the underdeveloped country for specialization. The human resources base for science and technology in underdeveloped countries is rather limited, and probably constitutes the main bottleneck for scientific and technological development. To overcome this limitation it is necessary to implement measures that would produce results: in the short term, programs such as the repatriation of qualified personnel working abroad; in the medium term, programs to expose professionals and scientists to advances in modern science and technology; and also in the long term, changes in the educational system. Financial and physical resources must also be increased, although there appears to be a greater need for a more rational use of existing funds and facilities for science and technology.

Incorporation of Technological Considerations in Development Planning

The third group of changes is oriented toward making science and technology an integral part of development planning (see Chapters 2 and 3). The first task consists in making planners and politicians aware of the role that science and technology play in the development process, emphasizing that technological domination reinforces underdevelopment. It is also necessary to show them that development plans and policies often contain negative implicit policies for science and technology, which make development efforts self-defeating in the long run.

The concern for scientific and technological policy making and planning is of relatively recent origin. As a consequence, there are no proven and accepted methods and criteria that could be recommended and applied with confidence.[22] Therefore, another task of high priority is the development of, and experimentation with, procedures for scientific and technological policy making and planning. The scientific method itself should be brought to bear in planning the development of science and technology. The awareness by planners and politicians of the importance of science and technology for development, and the availability of adequate methods for scientific and technological planning, would combine to legitimize the incorporation of science and technology within the scope of overall development planning efforts.

The three groups of changes described above amount to a radical transformation of the world scientific and technological effort. On the basis of past history, it is highly improbable that these changes will come about automatically. If they are realized, they will be the result of purposeful action by those who stand to gain from them. Therefore, this transformation must be pressed and started by the underdeveloped countries themselves.

However, it is rather unlikely that individual country efforts to modify the international division of labor in science and technology, as well as the norms that regulate the behavior of the international scientific community, will bear fruit in the short and medium terms. In consequence, underdeveloped countries should begin by organizing their own limited efforts, by augmenting their own capacity in science and technology, and by joining forces to initiate the transformation. In the last analysis, this is the only way in which the future of underdeveloped countries will be in their own hands.

NOTES

1. Celso Furtado, Development and Underdevelopment (Los Angeles: University of California Press, 1962).

2. Oswaldo Sunkel and Pedro Paz, El Subdesarrollo Latinoamericano y la Teoría del Desarrollo (México: Siglo XXI Editores, 1970).

3. François Perroux, L'Economie du XXème Siècle (Paris: Presses Universitaires de France, 1961). See also Jorge Bravo Bresani, Desarrollo y Subdesarrollo (Lima: Moncloa Editores, 1967).

4. For an elaboration of these concepts see J. Bravo Bresani, A. Salazar Bondy, and Francisco Sagasti, El Reto del Perú en la Perspectiva del Tercer Mundo (Lima: Moncloa-Campodonico Editores, 1972); and G. O'Donnell and Delfina Linck, Dependencia y Autonomía (Buenos Aires: Amorrortu Editores, 1974).

5. Oscar Lange, Ensayos sobre Planificación Económica (Barcelona: Ariel, 1970), p. 55.

6. Two reports are particularly important in this regard: Ignacy Sachs et al., Le changement technologique comme variable des politiques de développement (Paris: Centre International de Recherche sur l'environnement et le développement [CIRED], 1974); idem., Technologies appropriées pour le Tiers Monde: vers un gestion du pluralisme technologique (Paris: CIRED, 1974).

7. Ashok Parthasarathi (rapporteur), "The Role of Self-Reliance in Alternative Development Strategies," in Pugwash on Self-reliance, ed. Wilbert Chagula, Bernard Feld, and Ashok Parthasarathi (New Delhi: Ankur Publishing House, 1977).

8. See Raymond Vernon, ed., The Technology Factor in International Trade (New York: Columbia University Press, 1970); and Harry Johnson, Technology and International Trade (London: St. Martin's, 1975).

9. Sussex Group, Science Technology and Underdevelopment: The Case for Reform. Science Policy Research Unit, Sussex University, 1970.

10. Ward Morehause and John Sigurdson, "Science, Technology and Poverty: The Issues Underlying the 1979 World Conference and Science and Technology for Development," Bulletin of Atomic Scientists (December 1977), pp. 21-28.

11. Charles Cooper and François Chesnais, "La Ciencia y la Tecnología en la Integración Europea," in Integración Política y Económica, ed. Oswaldo Sunkel (Santiago de Chile: Editorial Universitaria, 1970); Organization for Economic Cooperation and Development (OECD), The Overall Level and Structure of R & D Efforts in OECD Member Countries (Paris: 1964); Harold Orlans, "D & R Allocations in the United States," Science Studies 3 (April 1973): 119-60; and H. Townsed, "Big Business and Big Science," Science and Public Policy 1 (October 1974): 290-97.

12. See, among other reports, Japanese Government, White Paper on Science and Technology. Spanish translation in Comercio Exterior, Mexico, February 1971.

13. Constantine Vaitsos, Strategic Choices in the Commercialization of Technology: The Point of View of Developing Countries (Lima: Junta del Acuerdo de Cartagena [JUNAC], 1970).

14. Gastón Oxman and Francisco Sagasti, La Transferencia de Tecnología hacia los Países del Grupo Andino (Washington, D.C.: Departamento de Asuntos Científicos, OEA, 1972).

15. Ignacy Sachs, La Découverte du Tiers Monde (Paris: Flammarion, 1971).

16. Sussex Group, op. cit.

17. Michael Polanyi, "The Republic of Science," in Criteria for Scientific Development, Public Policy and National Goals, ed. Edward Shils (Cambridge, Mass.: MIT Press, 1969).

18. Sussex Group, op. cit.

19. United Nations, Science and Technology for Development (New York: United Nations, 1971). Summary of the World Plan of Action on Science and Technology for the UN Second Development Decade.

20. Alvin Weinberg, "Criteria for Scientific Choice," in Criteria for Scientific Development, Public Policy and National Goals, ed. Edward Shils (Cambridge, Mass.: MIT Press, 1969).

21. Francisco Sagasti and Mauricio Guerrero, El Desarrollo Científico y Tecnológico de América Latina (Buenos Aires: Banco Interamericano de Desarrollo/Instituto de Integración de America Latina [BID/INTAL], 1974).

22. Reviews of available planning methods for science and technology can be found in: Organization for Economic Co-operation and Development, Analytical Methods in Government Science Policy (Paris: OECD, 1970); and Francisco Sagasti, A Review and Critique of Approaches and Methods Proposed for Scientific and Technological Planning (Washington, D.C.: Department of Scientific Affairs, OAS, 1970).

2

Science and Technology Planning in Underdeveloped Countries

THE CONTEXT OF SCIENCE AND TECHNOLOGY PLANNING

In the broadest sense, planning is anticipatory decision making. It consists in exerting choices in situations that have not yet occurred but that are envisioned to occur, that are interrelated and interdependent, and that are not known with certainty. The anticipatory decisions that constitute the planning process are concerned with the generation, identification, and evaluation of alternatives. Policy making can be distinguished from planning because it involves establishing the criteria for generating, identifying, and choosing among these alternatives. A planning methodology refers to the procedures followed in arriving at the commitments made in advance by the planners, and to the way in which they are translated into actual decisions. A plan consists of statements spelling out the anticipatory decisions taken, their interrelations, and the criteria employed in making them.[1] Scientific and technological (S and T) planning can thus be defined as the process of making anticipatory decisions about the development of science and technology and their insertion into the socioeconomic development process. The criteria for making such decisions are derived from science and technology policies, which in turn reflect, either explicitly or implicitly, the political will of government and the groups in power.

The growing attention that S and T planning has received during the past few years has distorted somewhat the perspective from which it should be viewed. Science and technology planning has

Used with permission from a paper presented at the STPI seminar on Science and Technology Planning, Villa de Leyva, Colombia, May 1975.

become a kind of mirage which disappears as soon as the harsh
political and budgetary realities are faced. Of course there are exceptions to this, and in some instances science and technology planners have been able to convert their visions into realities, at least
in part, but usually in a limited way and after bruising contact with
other actors in the political process.[2] When development planning
in general is not given great importance by the government, it is
obvious that S and T planning will be paid little attention. This may
be either because planning is marginal to the socioeconomic life of
the country or because the planning establishment--when it com-
mands attention and power--may not be inclined to consider science
and technology as a significant component of development planning.
But even when science and technology are considered important,
they usually are not awarded the same priority as other social and
economic activities. This may lead to a margination of science and
technology when resources are allocated in budgetary negotiations,
particularly in times of economic crisis.

Science and technology planning requires the active participation of the scientific and technological community, which usually
takes place under the stimulus of vague political commitments at the
highest levels of government. However, when other pressing issues
take precedence over science and technology, the scientific and
technological community becomes disenchanted with the S and T
planners, whom they see as failing to deliver their promises. This
may jeopardize the chances of engaging in the future in a meaningful
process of planning science and technology. Furthermore, there is
often a cleavage between the scientists of the "establishment," who
obtain resources and funds through their influence on particular departments, government agencies, foundations, or foreign organizations and who resist planning efforts, and the younger scientists and
engineers who see planning as a way of redistributing resources and
developing the science and technology system in a more organic
fashion and linked to development objectives. Thus S and T planners
must build and maintain a heterogeneous constituency in the face of
adverse environmental conditions.

These remarks are intended to place S and T planning within
the constraints under which it operates in the majority of underdeveloped countries, so that the discussions that follow will not be interpreted as giving science and technology planning more importance
than it really has. In the last analysis only the political will of government, if and when it can influence the behavior of the socioeconomic system, will legitimize S and T planning. The test for this is
whether, in the face of resource constraints and adverse political
pressures, science and technology planners are given enough political
support and resources to maneuver the development of science and
technology along the directions they establish.

ECONOMIC PLANNING AND S AND T PLANNING

At the outset it is necessary to establish a difference between planning scientific and technological activities and the integration of technology considerations into economic development planning. There is a body of what can be called scientific and technological activities, comprising basic research, adaptive research, development, engineering design, support activities such as information systems and special training courses, and so on. It is to these that the anticipatory decisions involved in science and technology planning are directed. Broadly speaking, they refer to the generation, importation, and absorption of technical knowledge.

Economic planning aims at orienting and regulating the activities of the productive system and the services related to it. From a particular structure of productive activities postulated by economic planners, it is possible to derive its technological implications and from these, in turn, to examine the types of scientific and technological activities required. The insertion of technological considerations in economic development planning involves both the explicit introduction of the technology issue at all phases of the planning process and the identification of implicit technology policies derived from the economic plans. To the extent that plans are implemented, these explicit and implicit aspects of technology in development planning shape the patterns of demand for technology.

Assuming that planning is taken seriously by the government, it will not suffice to devote attention to science and technology planning alone, for doing so would miss the essential component of the pattern of demand for S and T activities. Whether economic planning aims at defining the types of activities in which the state will be involved (through direct financing, allocation of credit, activities of state enterprises, and so on), or at regulating the activities of nongovernment sectors (primarily private industry), the resultant effect will be the adoption of an economic strategy that imbeds a technological strategy and defines technology needs.

The first task is to spell out the technological implications of the plan, pointing out the types of technology required (for example, to satisfy growth and employment targets), the constraints imposed by the projects selected, the technologies required to exploit natural resources, the technical demands imposed by export targets, and so on. A second stage aims at explicitly introducing technology as a strategic variable (in the same way as other multidimensional variables such as employment and financing) in the formulation of economic plans.[3]

As an illustrative example, Table 2.1 lists the types of technological considerations that could be introduced, taking the usual categories of long-, medium-, and short-term planning, as well as

TABLE 2.1

Technological Implications Derived from Economic Development Plans

Level	Term		
	Long	Medium	Short
Global	Formulation of technological styles closely linked to development styles and consumption patterns	Identification of general strategy, of priorities for the development of skills and capabilities, and of overall targets for resource allocation	Definition of total budget for S and T and project portfolio
Sectoral	Identification of the requirements to build up domestic capabilities in priority sectors	Definition of sectoral strategies and identification of programs for S and T activities	Definition of projects, activities, and budgets linked to sectoral strategies
Project	Assessment of the impact of investment projects and identification of technological constraints introduced (particularly for "heavy" projects)	Disaggregation of the technology package and identification of components to be supplied locally	Identification of firms and institutions to perform project-related activities (engineering design, adaptation, construction)

Note: The regional dimension would introduce variations due to specific environmental conditions.
Source: Compiled by the author.

the level of plans (global, sectoral, project). Another dimension that could be introduced is the regional, which would add spatial considerations to the issues being taken into account. The linkage between S and T planning and the incorporation of technology into economic planning takes place through several mechanisms, as can be easily inferred from the table. Each of the cells can be associated with a group of scientific and technological activities and hence will affect the process of scientific and technological planning.

ATTITUDES OF VARIOUS GROUPS TOWARD S AND T PLANNING

The different attitudes of scientists, engineers, planners, and politicians to S and T planning can be characterized in terms of three archetypes. They are rarely found in pure form in an individual or institution in underdeveloped countries, but they help to focus the types of conflicts that emerge in the planning process.[4]

Liberal Scientists

The first attitude to be considered is that of the liberal scientists, whose main interest is promoting the growth of science for its own sake. (Technology will follow automatically.) They resist any intervention in the conduct of scientific affairs as an infringement of the freedom of research. They distrust the concept of S and T planning and prefer to see the evolution of science as linked to the world system for the generation of knowledge. "Science has no frontiers" and "priorities must come from the evolution of science itself" are two of their favorite slogans. Liberal scientists can adopt a radical stance, rejecting any form of intervention in the orientation of the scientific activity, or a moderate one, accepting that there must be some kind of government intervention in expressing preferences for the types of activities they perform. Radical liberal scientists are becoming rare, although they can be found among older and renowned scientists who do not face difficulties in obtaining funds for research. Moderate liberal scientists usually assume leadership positions in the scientific community and their view is that government must support science, accepting in exchange general orientations, but that planning is not necessary and that with time the growth of the scientific activity will lead to the development of indigenous technology.

Technoeconomists

The technoeconomists view science, and technology in particular, as a means for accelerating socioeconomic development. For them, technology and the scientific activities that support it are essential components of a development strategy. They view government intervention as necessary to promote the growth of scientific and technological activities and emphasize the importance of national objectives in guiding the development of science and technology (rejecting the internationalist view of science). Technoeconomists may come in "pure" form, in which case they downplay the importance of scientific activities and favor technological activities alone; or they may see both science and technology as necessary, although placing more emphasis on technology and accepting science insofar as it constitutes a necessary input into technology. Technoeconomists are most frequently found among the young technocrats, politicians, and scientists who become involved in S and T planning.

Growth Advocates

The third archetypal attitude is that of the growth advocates. Whereas liberal scientists justify the pursuit of science in its own right and technoeconomists are concerned with the integration of science and technology into socioeconomic development, the growth advocates do not award science and technology any distinct roles of their own in the development process. They view technology as a mere input into the process of economic growth and do not care at all about its origin. Unlike the technoeconomists, they are not prepared to accept any postponement in the achievement of growth targets for the sake of developing local technological capabilities. Either through open hostility or benign neglect, growth advocates oppose the idea that the acquisition of an indigenous science and technology capacity is an integral component of the development process.

These different views and interests inevitably lead to conflicts in the process of science and technology planning, determining to a large extent the impact of the planning exercise. For example, growth advocates and liberal scientists often form a coalition against the technoeconomists, which results in abandoning technology considerations in development planning. The most that is done in this case is to allocate a certain amount of funds via established government channels, usually at the disposal of liberal scientists. In this case technoeconomists are squeezed out of the planning process and the S and T plan becomes an aggregate of research projects. Technoeconomists may gain the upper hand in some instances, but usually at the price of alienating the liberal scientists and irritating the growth advocates. Initially the liberal scientists may see some advantage in following the point of view of the technoeconomists, particularly because it may lead to additional sources of funds, but at a later stage they resist the degree of control that the technoeconomists see as necessary for linking scientific and technological activities to development objectives.

It is usually harder to find a community of interests between technoeconomists and growth advocates. This may be a reason that technology considerations have not become an integral part of economic planning. To the extent that S and T planning is seen as a separate exercise, growth advocate planners have no objection to it. Indeed, they may even welcome an extra section in a plan, one that deals with science and technology in the manner of the liberal scientists. However, when technology impinges on growth, as it must when being integrated into the economic plan, they reject it flatly. One familiar example of this controversy is shown when technological self-reliance is considered a legitimate development objective. The achievement of a moderate degree of technological self-reliance requires a learning process through the performance of engineering and research activities which may delay the completion of a project. This is anathema to the growth advocates, who would favor the complete importation of technology rather than face a delay.

S AND T PLANNING AND RESOURCE ALLOCATION

The margin for maneuver of the S and T planners is determined by their ability to direct the allocation of resources to science and technology. One approach to achieve this capability consists in consolidating into a science and technology budget the funds allocated by various government departments. This consolidation of funds may simply mean listing together in the same volume (or chapter) of the development plan (or budget) the appropriations made by different agencies and departments, showing their relation to wider development objectives. In this case S and T planners play merely a coordinating role with no power to interfere in the allocations made by the agencies; they suggest and induce rather than decide or execute.

A second way of influencing resource allocation is to establish a special fund, fed by government appropriations and managed by the S and T planners. This fund constitutes an additional source of financing for science and technology, complementing allocations made by other agencies. S and T planners thus acquire an executive capability, although their impact is conditioned by the relative magnitude of the special fund. At times of economic crisis the special fund will tend to shrink as the activities financed out of regular sources demand more financing. A variation on this approach consists in the special fund being fed out of directed appropriations which do not depend on budgetary negotiations. The resources may be obtained by establishing a tax or a cess on exports, credits, net income of enterprises, sales, and so on. When resources are obtained from contributions by enterprises, they can be managed in a centralized way, or by giving the contributors a say on the S and T programs to be supported. This approach grants the S and T planners more room to maneuver and widens their support base.*

The solution adopted by the S and T planners to influence resource allocation may involve the two approaches mentioned above. Certainly the coordinating role is important, but it may prove sterile unless reinforced by the capacity to intervene directly through the creation of one or more special funds.

THE CONTENT OF S AND T PLANNING

Science and technology planning is frequently confused with research planning. There is a tendency to ignore scientific and technological activities other than research when discussing S and T planning. Yet research may not be the most important component of the S and T plan, particularly in underdeveloped countries. Assuming that the planning process should lead to the identification of scientific and technological activities to be supported with priority in order to link science and technology development objectives, it is possible to identify activities related to the importation and absorption of technology (identification and evaluation of technological alternatives, regulation of the technology import process, engineering design, technology adaptation, experimentation in plants, and so on); to support of services (documentation centers, technical information and extension, education and training programs, and so on); and to the promotion of the demand for indigenous technology (use of incentives, of industrial credit, and so on) that should be awarded equal or more importance than research.

---

*This is the approach followed by the Peruvian government through a network of sectoral funds and research institutes. See Chapter 7.

There are many ways of defining and classifying scientific and technological activities. [5] One that appears to be fruitful because it spans both S and T planning and the insertion of technology into development planning, is to divide them into activities related to the promotion of demand for indigenous technology, to the absorption of technology, to the regulation of imported technology, to the production of technology, and to the supporting services (primarily information and training). Given that these five categories are primarily linked to technology, a sixth category comprising basic and curiosity-oriented research should be added. Within each category further subdivisions can be introduced (by problem area, discipline, sector, type of activity, and so on) providing the overall spectrum of scientific and technological activities to be considered in the planning process.

Although science and technology planning covers activities that are considered part of science and those that belong to the realm of technology, it is clear that the differences between the two require that they be treated in different ways. Thus, under the overall umbrella of science and technology planning and policy making, it is possible to distinguish between the set of criteria for anticipatory decision making associated with science and that associated with technology, giving rise to a science policy and technology policy that are integrated within the framework of S and T planning (see Chapter 5).

The anticipatory decisions contained in science and technology plans have been usually related to the definition of scientific and technological activities and the allocation of resources. The concept that a plan is a collection of projects has prevailed in the majority of S and T planning exercises, which has led to a neglect of other issues involved in relating science and technology to development objectives. The most important among these are the anticipatory decisions regarding the institutional structure for the performance of scientific and technological activities, the patterns of interaction with the economic and educational systems, and the definition of a desired image or style for the development of science and technology. The content of S and T planning should be expanded to incorporate considerations of this type. (These concepts are elaborated further in Chapter 3.)

THE ORGANIZATION OF THE S AND T PLANNING EFFORT

The process of arriving at the anticipatory decisions that constitute S and T planning imposes certain organizational requirements.

Because of their participatory nature most of these exercises have adopted the same structure, consisting of a coordinating group with an executive secretariat, assisted by a number of technical committees. These committees are usually integrated by researchers, staff members of the S and T planning agency, and in some cases by engineers and users of the results of S and T activities. They may be vertical--dealing with a particular sector, problem area, or discipline--or horizontal--cutting across these divisions and dealing with issues such as human resources, information, and policy instruments.* The variations found among different planning exercises arise out of the power and mandate of the central coordinating group; the number, type, and composition of the committees; the mandate given by the central groups to the committees; and the degree of intervention of the central group and the committees in the implementation of the plan.

The relation of the coordinating group to the central planning agency may be one of subordination, with S and T planners being part of the central planning agency and reporting to it. More frequently, the S and T planning group is given, at least formally, equal status with the economic planners and thus the S and T plan is supposedly coordinated with the economic plan. However, even when equal status is granted to S and T planning, the disparity in resources, political access, and power relegates it to a secondary position.

The number of committees set up by the coordinating group usually exceeds the number of departments in the government. Leaving aside the defense departments (S and T planning normally covers civil science and technology only), a certain number of sectoral committees correspond roughly to the structure of public administration. These are complemented by committees dealing with special problem areas (energy, water resources, and so on), with basic science (usually subdivided by disciplines), and with horizontal issues such as human resources and measures to enhance the productivity of research organizations. The structure may involve several hundred participants.

Differences among S and T planning exercises arise to a large extent out of the composition of the technical committees. The scientific community may dominate the membership, the majority of committee members may belong to government departments, or there may be a balanced representation of planners and administrators,

---

*This approach has been followed in practice by countries as varied as Brazil, India, Mexico, Egypt, Korea, Colombia, and Venezuela.

of scientists and engineers, and of users of the results of science and technology. The implementation of the plan depends on such balance because scientific and technological activities cannot be carried out through imposition and the use of their results cannot be forced, which requires that those in charge of making the transition from anticipatory to actual decisions be involved in all phases of the planning process.

The committees may be given a high degree of autonomy to define strategies, priorities, resource allocation, and even specific projects from the beginning, limiting the role of the central group to one of assembling their proposals. When such a broad mandate is given to the committees it is almost certain that the S and T plan will result in a collection of projects defined after hard bargaining among committee members. Another approach gives each committee, under strong central guidance, the task of defining first a strategy for the sector, problem area, or discipline of its competence, outlining areas of concentration and general priorities. After a first revision and integration of committee programs, the coordinating group may ask the committees to review their programs within a framework of maximum and minimum levels of resource availabilities. At this stage the committees may be asked to outline specific research projects to be contracted out, or the scientific and technological community may be invited to present projects in accordance with the programs. [6]

The degree of intervention of the central group and the committees in the implementation of the plan will depend on the relative power of the science and technology planners and on the resources at their disposal, particularly in relation to the traditional ways of channeling funds to scientific and technological activities through government departments. If and when the plan is put into practice the committees may be given the task of monitoring its progress in their fields of competence. When no role is reserved for the committees after formulating the plan, they may be disbanded, in which case monitoring becomes a function of the central coordinating group. For some important problem areas or issues that require attention over a long period, permanent committees may be set up under the aegis of the S and T planners and the corresponding government agencies.

THE LIMITS OF S AND T PLANNING METHODS

There exists a relatively large number of formal methods and procedures devised to help the science and technology planners in the definition of priorities and the allocation of resources, particularly for research activities. Most of them have been used in demonstration exercises, and only a handful have been applied in real situations.[7] The general impression left by a careful study of the available methods is that formalizations and theory run well ahead of practice in science and technology planning. Most of the quantitative methods require a wealth of data and introduce many assumptions that simplify the problems to the point of triviality. There is a manifest need for a systematic framework for the analysis of such methods and the value they may have for science and technology planning.

In addition to the shortcomings inherent in the planning methods, S and T planners often compound the problem by expecting too much from methodologies. This gives rise to a technocratic dream in which the S and T planners can plug data into a model in order to define priorities, resource levels, and projects. In practice this never happens.

With regard to the identification of priorities, there are a few heuristic rules which may provide some guidance. The first is to diversify as much as possible the sources of priorities, examining initiatives from the scientific and technological community, problem areas posed by the users, government policies contained in the plan, invariant problems that will remain important for long periods, areas arising out of short-term social or economic problems, and so on. Priorities for scientific and technological activities should be determined through an interplay of various forces, rather than through the expression of the planners' views and biases.

The second heuristic rule is to avoid treating the development plan as the primary source of priorities for science and technology. There is no automatic relation between economic development priorities and S and T priorities. Their time horizons are different, and giving too much importance to the development plan may lead to ignoring key contributions that science and technology can make to development. In effect, there are probably many projects that are not included in the development plan precisely because the scientific and technical knowledge to perform them is not available. If priorities for S and T are extracted from the plan alone, then the necessary knowledge may never be developed.

Determining the appropriate level of resource allocation for a sector, problem area, or discipline has been a perennial problem of S and T planners. Actual allocations in the case of existing activities are bounded at the upper level by the absorption capacity of the S and T system, and at the lower level by the minimum necessary to continue the programs. In the case of new activities, the limits are difficult to establish, although they can be related to the possibility of assembling a team of scientists and professionals that may absorb the resources without undue waste.

CONCLUSION

Science and technology planning efforts in underdeveloped countries are just beginning. They have not been fully legitimized as yet and confront the double opposition of liberal scientists and growth advocates. Therefore, S and T planners face an uphill battle in the process of introducing technology considerations into the development planning process, and in orienting the conduct of scientific and technological activities. To perform these tasks adequately it is necessary to pay attention to the organization of the planning exercise, and to devise practical operational procedures that can bring down to earth the multiplicity of sophisticated methodologies that have been suggested.

NOTES

1. For a more detailed exposition of these concepts see Francisco Sagasti, "A Conceptual Systems' Framework for the Study of Planning Theory," Technological Forecasting and Social Change 5 (1973): 379-93.

2. For a thorough discussion of these problems see Francisco Sagasti and Alberto Araoz, eds., Science and Technology Planning in Less Developed Countries: The Experience of the STPI Countries (Ottawa: IDRC, 1978).

3. See, for example, Ignacy Sachs and Krystina Vinaver, Integration of Technology in Development Planning, report submitted to the Field Coordinator's Office, STPI Project, January 1976. Reprinted in Sagasti and Araoz, eds., op. cit.

4. See Robert Seidel, Towards an Andean Common Market for Science and Technology (Ithaca, N.Y.: Cornell University Press, 1974).

5. For definitions of scientific and technological activities adapted to the needs of less developed countries, see Resumen de estudios sobre política tecnológica (Lima: Junta del Acuerdo de Cartagena, 1973); Francisco Sagasti, A Systems Approach to Science and Technology Policy Making and Planning (Washington, D.C.: Department of Scientific Affairs, OAS, 1972).

6. A highly imaginative and successful exercise of this type is reported in a paper by James Brian Quinn and Robert Major, "Norway: A Small Country Plans Civil Science and Technology," Science 183 (1974): 172-79.

7. See Marvin Centron and Joel Goldhar, eds., The Science of Managing Organized Technology (New York: Gordon and Breach, 1970); Francisco Sagasti, A Systems Approach to Science and

Technology Policy Making and Planning (Washington, D.C.: Department of Scientific Affairs, OAS, 1972); and Claude Maestre and Keith Pavitt, Analytical Methods in Government Science Policy (Paris: OECD, 1971). Wolfgang Mostert has prepared an annotated review of the literature, La planificación de la ciencia y technologia en los paises en desarrollo (Lima, Peru: Escuela Superior de Administración de Negocios [ESAN], 1976).

3

Anticipatory Decisions Involved in Science and Technology Planning

CATEGORIES OF DECISIONS IN PLANNING

Since anticipatory decisions are the building blocks of planning, the development of planning methods should consider explicitly the different types of such decisions that have to be made, for these may require different types of planning procedures. Five general categories of decisions can be identified in the process of planning for scientific and technological development: first, decisions that will define long-term ideals and the desired future image of the system; second, decisions regarding the pattern of interactions with related systems and their decision areas; third, decisions about the institutional infrastructure of the system; fourth, decisions to determine the scope and nature of the activities to be performed by the system; and fifth, decisions on the allocation of all types of resources These five anticipatory decision categories are the domains of stylistic, contextual, institutional, activity, and resource planning, respectively. The interactions among these categories of decisions can be summarized by saying that resources are allocated to activities through institutions, taking into account the context in order to approach the desired future.

However, even if a conceptual and operational separation of these five types of planning activities is possible, it must be emphasized that they are not independent and that they cannot be dealt with separately and individually. A planning methodology that will simultaneously identify the combination of activities, the institutional structure, and the allocation of resources that optimize the performance of the system—making it approach its ideal—is what

Used with permission from a paper published in Social Sciences Information 12 (1973): 67-95.

planners would like to have at their disposal. Unfortunately, it is rather unlikely that such a methodology can be developed in the near future, and the most viable alternative appears to be the development of iterative planning procedures that take each category of decisions in turn, defining a provisional plan to be revised once anticipatory decisions have been made in the other areas.

These five categories for scientific and technological planning can be regarded as a framework within which to order the tasks involved in planning for scientific and technological development. Current planning methods refer only to the categories of activity and resource planning; there are no methods specifically designed for anticipatory decision making in any of the three other categories.

The different characteristics of anticipatory decisions in each of the five categories impose the need for developing different planning paradigms—conceived as the collection of points of view, habits of thought, methods, and models—for the five different categories of planning activities. Planning concepts, procedures, and methods that are appropriate for one planning category cannot be expected to be equally appropriate and applicable to any of the other categories, which differ in almost every respect. For example, resource planning procedures and the resource perspective of planning cannot be applied effectively in institutional, contextual, and stylistic planning. The particular problems of resource distribution and allocation have little in common with those of institutional building, those of coordinating policies and plans, and those of designing the ideal desired future. Hence, it becomes necessary to discard old thinking habits when moving from one category of planning to another. These remarks can be put forward in the form of a principle: planning for scientific and technological development should consider the different categories of planning decisions that have to be made and develop approaches and methods appropriate for each.

The different characteristics of the five types of anticipatory decisions described above suggest that they may fall within the domains of different planning organizations. Assuming the existence of a central agency in charge of scientific and technological planning, stylistic planning would then be performed by the planning agency and the interest groups that are in one way or another affected by the anticipatory decisions to be taken. Contextual planning would be a task to be performed by the planning agency in conjunction with planning agencies in other related systems. Institutional, activity, and resource planning would be carried out by the planning agency and the other institutions and organizations acting within the boundaries of the scientific and technological system.

The relationships between the different categories of planning and the three time dimensions of long-, medium-, and short-range planning can be outlined as follows: stylistic planning is essentially a long-range planning activity, and the dimensions of medium and short range are not relevant to it. Contextual, institutional, and activity planning are seen to be primarily medium-range planning activities, although the identification of ideal patterns of interaction, institutional structures, and patterns of activities would be included within stylistic planning and hence become part of a long-range planning exercise. The dimension of short-term planning appears to be less important for these three planning categories. Finally, resource planning involves the three time dimensions considered, although it is primarily oriented to short-range planning. Occasionally long- and medium-term resource commitments have to be made, but by and large resource planning is concerned with short-range considerations through the budgetary process. Summarizing, it may be said that the short range is the dominant time dimension for resource planning, that the medium range is the dominant time dimension for activity, institutional, and contextual planning, and that the long range is the dominant time dimension for stylistic planning.

The main characteristics of the five types of planning activities are summarized in Table 3.1. The conditioning factors, the areas where emphasis is placed, the type of process and the procedures involved, the organizations responsible for carrying them out, and the dominant time horizon are specified for each of the five types or categories of planning activity.

STYLISTIC PLANNING

The general objectives of stylistic planning are to project a desired future image of the scientific and technological system as an ideal to be approached, and to engage the participation of the interested groups affected by planning, exposing their values and preferences in the process. The stylistic plan is turned into an instrument to promote dialogue and participation, rather than being the justification of the planning activity. The main outcome of the process becomes a common view of the future and a perspective shared by those participating in the process, rather than a description of the plan by the statements contained in the documents.

Eric Trist,[1] commenting on Michael Crozier's analysis of French economic planning, has emphasized that the learning process that takes place during the preparation of a plan is far more important than the plan itself. Suggestions by James Caroll[2] point out

TABLE 3.1

Characteristics of the Different Categories of Planning Decisions

	Stylistic	Contextual	Institutional	Activity	Resource
Conditioning influences	Value systems and preferences (stylistic constraints); long-term possibilities	Environmental constraints; interdependencies with other systems	Institutional constraints and possibilities for development; organizational ecology	Existing and potential capabilities; dynamics of processes	Availability of resources; possibilities for directing allocations
Emphasis	Alternative futures; desired image (willed future); clarification of values	convergence of different policies and plans; attaining overall coherence in plans and policies	Establishing appropriate organizational structures (channels and clusters)	Defining areas for concentration of activities; evaluation of past performance	Influencing resource allocation
Type of process	Exploratory; consultative; multiple-loop	Coordinating; negotiative	Structuring and texturing (setting the organizational fabric)	Diagnosing; target-setting; balancing; learning	Allocative and distributive; experimental
Procedures used	Establishing ideal standards; proposing broad directions; establishing dialogue with interest groups	Making explicit relevant implicit policies; resolving contradictions; use of indirect instruments for implementing plans and policies	Institution building and renewal (creation and modification of institutions); defining performance measures; setting the "rules of the game"	Establishing objectives; defining orientation; setting operational procedures	Acquiring and distributing resources; establishing priorities for resource allocation; defining specific aims and goals; generating a data base
Decision makers	Planning agency and interest groups	Planning agency and agencies in other systems	Planning agency and other organizations in the system	Planning agency and other organizations in the system	Planning agency and other organizations in the system
Dominant time horizon	Long-range	Medium-range	Medium-range	Medium-range	Short-range

Source: Compiled by the author.

that this learning process and the involvement generated by participatory forms of planning, particularly in technological matters,
need not be confined to the immediately interested parties, such as
the government and scientists, but can also spread to ordinary
citizens. Therefore, participation and dialogue with all interested
parties to identify the style in which the system would evolve, while
at the same time initiating a learning process, become the main
concerns of this planning category.

Stylistic planning is an exploratory multiple-loop process
conditioned primarily by value structures and preferences, which
Russell Ackoff[3] calls "stylistic constraints." It puts emphasis on
the specification of alternative futures and the definition of a desired image or a "willed future."[4] The ideal future image of the
system to be designed in stylistic planning must include statements
on the patterns of interdependence with other related systems. For
example, it should specify the possible contributions of science and
technology to economic and educational development, and to the
use of natural resources. It should also contain a description of
the ideal institutional infrastructure for the system, the structure
of activities to be performed, and the ideal pattern of resource
acquisition and allocation.

The image of the desired future would be put forward in terms
of scenarios consisting of qualitative statements about the characteristics of the system and its interrelations with the environment
at a certain future time. The scenarios would be complemented by
proposals regarding the general strategy to be followed in order to
approach the ideal state they describe. The statements need not be
quantitative or supported by detailed projections; initially they
should be impressionistic descriptions of the scientific and technological system at some time in the future. As the interactions
in the continuous process of stylistic planning evolve, these scenarios would be refined and brought in focus more clearly, to take
into account possible developments in the system and external
limitations.[5]

The time horizon for stylistic planning is long-range, and
consists of a span of time long enough so that the present situation
and its dynamics do not condition to any significant extent the future
situation. This does not imply, however, that questions of possibility and feasibility are completely discarded.

The concern for the design of ideal future systems is not a
recent one. In addition to traditional utopian thinking (Plato, St.
Augustine, Sir Thomas More, and so on), the design of ideal systems has been advocated on the basis of its contributions to actual
decision making at the practical level. Perhaps one of the most
coherent early descriptions of the possible use of ideal schemes

for taking action was given by Piotr Kropotkin in 1873, in an essay titled "Must we occupy ourselves with an examination of the ideal of a future system?"

> I believe that we must. In the first place, in the ideal we can express our hopes, aspirations and goals, regardless of practical limitations, regardless of the degree of realization which we may attain; for this degree of realization is determined purely by external causes.
>
> In the second place, the ideal can make clear how much we are infected with old prejudices and inclinations. If some aspects of everyday life seem to us so sacred that we dare not touch them even in an analysis of the ideal, then how great will our daring be in the actual abolishment of these everyday features? In other words, although daring in thought is not at all a guarantee of daring in practice, mental timidity in constructing an ideal is certainly a criterion of mental timidity in practice.[6]

Kropotkin stresses the benefits of freeing the imagination from questions of feasibility in order to uncover latent value structures and preferences. In a different vein, both Ackoff[7] and Ozbekhan[8] have emphasized the same benefits that can be derived from such an exercise in utopian thinking. Ackoff proposes the construction of scenarios that are bounded only by stylistic constraints, and Ozbekhan suggests the design of a willed future embodying only preference and value considerations. However, ideal future images, to be of real benefit in stylistic planning, must be tempered in some way by the concept of what it is possible to achieve.

The view of the future implicit in stylistic planning is purposeful and interventionist. It involves the design of a future rather than the extrapolation of current trends and existing conditions, or the projection of most likely developments based on extrapolations and the potential reactive responses to them. The extrapolated view of the future can be conceptualized in terms of the statement, "If present trends continue and no action is taken, then the future will look like this." The most likely or "surprise-free" view of the future agrees with the statement, "Given current trends, and the fact that this or that action will probably be taken in reaction, then the future is most likely to look like this."

The stylistic view of the future adopts a wishful and purposeful stance; it seeks to design the future as one would like it to be, to express concrete aspirations in the form of an ideal future state, and then to devise a strategy for reaching it, given present conditions. Initially, the questions of feasibility and possibility should be avoided for the reasons that Kropotkin suggests; namely, they should not interfere with the vision of the future which could bring new ideas and would embody preferences and values; but these questions need to be introduced when modifying the desired image and devising a strategy for attaining it. At later stages the extrapolated and most likely futures should play the role of "reference projections" with which to compare the desired future. From this comparison, Ackoff's "planning gap" emerges, and the planners are confronted with the void between the projected and desired futures which has to be filled through purposeful action.

The questions of feasibility and actual possibilities introduce a balancing force for the utopian thinking involved in the design of desired future. In stylistic planning for science and technology this is done in two ways: through the preparation of a diagnosis of the existing situation, its dynamics, and its possibilities for future development; and through the use of technological forecasting to examine the feasibility of attaining particular aspects of the desired future image, ascertaining whether the levels of effort required are commensurate with potentialities.

The injection of a measure of reality into the stylistic planning process is designed to avoid the temptation to embrace the concepts and statements contained in a purely wishful desired future, elaborate on them, and then assume the desired image to be an accomplished fact. This tendency has been called "projectismo" and has been identified as a characteristic of much planning in the Third World. Bertram Gross suggests that this is a feature common to planning in many underdeveloped countries where

> dreams are easy to concoct but the conflicts and obstacles to achievement are tremendous. . . .
>
> Projectismo is based upon utopian commitments to a desired situation that are simply impossible to obtain. In this latter case, the elaboration of presumed methods of attaining the unattainable may serve to make the plan more plausible, even though not a bit more feasible. Yet the fact that a plan may be utopian need not prevent its reaching the stage of central decision and commitment. National political leaders often make "pie in the sky" promises as the only way to distract attention from current suffering. [9]

Therefore, by introducing a diagnosis of the existing and potential capabilities in science and technology and incorporating technological forecasting within the scope of stylistic planning for science and technology, it may be possible to avoid the pitfalls that are associated with purely utopian and wishful thinking in the design of a desired future image.

There are reasons that suggest that the process of building a planning capability, particularly in science and technology, should give priority to stylistic planning. Being a long-range planning exercise, it affects resource, activity, institutional, and contextual planning more than they affect it. Furthermore, planners, policy makers, and other interested groups find it easier to agree on long-term ideal conceptualizations than on short-term problems of resource allocation or medium-term problems of defining activities, building institutions, and coordinating with other systems. Stylistic planning may thus provide a basis for agreement which would be otherwise difficult to obtain.

CONTEXTUAL PLANNING

The second category of planning decisions refers to the pattern of interaction between the scientific and technological system and its interrelated systems in the environment. Contextual planning is concerned with attaining coherence among these interacting systems, and with exploring the possibility of using indirect instruments and mechanisms for implementing planning decisions. It is conditioned by environmental constraints and lays emphasis on the convergence of policies and plans put forward by different systems, primarily through coordination and negotiation processes. The procedures it follows involve making explicit the consequences of other systems' policies and plans, resolving contradictions that may appear among them, and analyzing possible ways of implementing scientific and technological plans through measures taken in other systems.

Interactions with the environment of the scientific and technological system are the main focus of contextual planning. The environment can be defined as those systems and their components that affect the behavior and performance of the scientific and technological system, but over which it has no possibility of exerting direct control. However, this does not imply that the system cannot influence the behavior of its environment. The negotiation and coordination processes referred to in the preceding paragraph are the means through which the behavior of other systems in the environment can be influenced without having direct control over them. Because of their importance for contextual planning, the characteristics of the environment merit further analysis.

Trist, in his contribution to a United Nations report on administrative capabilities for development, proposes a differentiation between the task and contextual environments of a system or organization:

It is necessary to distinguish between the immediate, operational or task environment and the more remote general or contextual environment. The task environment consists of all organizations, groups and people with whom the organization has specific relations, on both the input and output sides, even though it may not be aware of their complete range. The contextual environment consists of the relations which the entities included in the task environment have to each other and to other systems not directly entering the world of the organization's own transactions. Events in the contextual environment may at any time obtrude into this world, constructively or destructively, predictably or unpredictably.[10]

For a system to deal effectively with its environment it is not sufficient to pay attention to the task environment, which is formed by the organizations, institutions, interest groups, and clients that have direct linkages with the system. It is also necessary to assess the potential influence of the contextual environment, seeking to anticipate changes that may affect the behavior of the system. For the scientific and technological system, the relations between different components of the economic system, those between the physico-ecological and the economic systems, those between the educational and economic systems, and so on, constitute the contextual environment.

In planning patterns of interaction it may be the case that some aspects and components of the contextual environment, particularly those which intrude on and affect the system's behavior and performance, need to be made part of the task environment by establishing direct links between them and the system. This may be thought of as a process of enlarging the scope and the influence of both actual and anticipatory decision making for the scientific and technological system.

The characteristics of the environment and of the policies made by the systems it contains constitute, in fact, a set of implicit policies for science and technology. Government economic and educational policies, in particular, contain an array of consequences or implicit policies that regulate the behavior of the scientific and technological system in an indirect way. These implicit science and technology policies must be made explicit if planning for scientific and technological development is to be effective. The process of making them explicit is likely to uncover contradictions and inconsistencies between overt objectives and policies and those forced on the system by its environment. The ways in which these contradictions are resolved will have a decisive influence on the future developments of science and technology.

The process of uncovering implicit policies and exposing contradictions is likely to lead to value conflicts. Contradictory policies are not made congruent simply by showing discordances and divergencies. These value conflicts must be resolved through coordination or negotiation; extreme cases may even require an open fight in order to determine the values and objectives that will prevail in the conflict. Once these conflicts are exposed in contextual planning, policy makers and planners will have to make choices overtly and with full knowledge of the value conflicts involved.

Therefore, contextual planning is concerned with the interdependencies between the system and its environment. It examines the implicit policies that are the consequences of actual and anticipatory decisions taken in other systems, it identifies contradictions and points out the ways of resolving them, and it also considers the possibility of using indirect instruments for implementing the system's policies and plans. Contextual planning constitutes primarily a medium-range activity; the existing situation, particularly with regard to the task and contextual environment, conditions the anticipatory decisions that will be taken, but does not determine them to a large extent.

INSTITUTIONAL PLANNING

The anticipatory decisions on institutional structure, which are the subject of institutional planning, refer to the organizational network through which activities are to be carried out and resources channeled, and to the rules and regulations which govern the behavior of the different units comprising the institutional infrastructure. Institutional planning is conditioned primarily by organizational constraints and the possibilities for institutional development; this is the organizational ecology of the scientific and technological system. It emphasizes the establishment of organizational and institutional channels and clusters, through a process of structuring and texturing which defines the organizational fabric of the system. The procedures followed in this type of planning activity include institution building and renewal, which refer to the creation and modification of institutions, setting the codes of behavior or "rules of the game," and defining the performance measures for organizations in the scientific and technological system.

The development of an institutional infrastructure for the scientific and technological system is a necessary condition for the development of science and technology in underdeveloped countries. René Maheu, former director general of the United Nations Education, Science and Culture Organization (UNESCO), in an address to a meeting of Southeast Asian countries, emphasized the importance of the network of institutions.

> The scientifically advanced nations know well—and this is precisely the secret of their technological pre-eminence— that the social and economic benefits derived from oriented or applied research depend on the existence and efficiency of what is known as the country's "operational network of scientific and technological research institutions."[11]

This network of institutions is generally well developed in advanced countries, and therefore they have seldom dealt with it explicitly. Planners in developed nations take the institutional structure for granted and address themselves to the problems of priorities or resource allocation. The fact that institutional structures are more developed in advanced countries has often led to the belief that underdeveloped countries should follow a strategy of imitation in planning their institutional development. William F. Whyte points out that this has been the case in Peru:

> There is a widespread tendency in Peru to imitate the institutional structure and practices of industrialized nations and to accept the institutions in other countries as standards against which Peruvian institutions are measured. Peruvians are self-conscious of their imitative tendencies, and we often hear nationalistic condemnation of outside influences and vigorous defense of what is Peruvian. But even those who express themselves in public most nationalistically, in private and casual conversation, talk about the inadequacies of Peru and Peruvians and the need for changing Peruvian institutions in the image of those of another country.[12]

This tendency toward institutional imitation has been responsible for several deficiencies found in Peruvian institutions, particularly in the fields of health care, higher education, industrial development, and even science and technology.

A strategy of institutional imitation is likely to fail and should be avoided for the following reasons. First, the context and the environment in which institutions operate in a developed country are widely different from those prevailing in the underdeveloped ones, and there is no guarantee that the institutions will operate efficiently and contribute to development. Second, if they had the choice, developed countries would probably prefer in many cases to develop institutional structures different from the ones they presently have, which are being copied. Third, the particular social and historical conditions of the underdeveloped country may provide opportunities to develop new institutional patterns that are better suited to local conditions, and that could eventually become models for other countries, underdeveloped and developed.

In underdeveloped countries the growth and evolution of institutions in the scientific and technological system have been slow. Research organizations, universities, research councils, and service organizations have lacked financial resources and qualified manpower, and in some cases, particularly in Latin America, there has been little demand for the knowledge and services they produce.

A well-organized institutional structure, particularly at the national level, cannot be developed from scratch in a short period of time. However inadequate, usually there is a core of institutions (even if they exist only on paper) from which to begin institution building and designing the organizational fabric in underdeveloped countries. Institutional planning takes the existing structure as a basis, examines it critically and proposes changes and additions to it. Once proposals are implemented, they should be left to evolve without changing them again too soon. A certain lead time is required to permit the institutions to stabilize after introducing major modifications, and frequent radical changes may retard the development of the institutional structure.

It is impossible to optimize an institutional design in the traditional sense. As far as can be determined, there are no proposed criteria for identifying and generating optimal institutional designs, particularly for the scientific and technological systems in underdeveloped countries. One possible strategy for generating and choosing among alternative institutional designs may be based on a "satisfycing" approach in which minimal conditions are established for an acceptable institutional structure. The selection among designs which satisfy the minimal conditions would be left outside the scope of institutional planning.

The satisfycing strategy can be improved by adding a second set of criteria based on the institutional design's capability for adjusting to changes in the system or its environment. This would constitute a "satisfying-adaptivizing" strategy[13] for institutional planning in which organizations and institutions are designed to comply with two sets of criteria: minimal standards that determine acceptability, and a set of conditions that would ensure the institution's capacity for adaptation. However, it may not be possible always to define the adaptability criteria in addition to the minimal set of standards the institutional design should satisfy.[14]

ACTIVITY PLANNING

Activity planning is concerned with the category of decisions referring to the scope and nature of activities to be performed by the system. It is conditioned by the existing and potential capabilities of the system and the dynamics of the processes taking place within its boundaries. Activity planning puts emphasis on the definition of priorities for concentrating activities and also on the evaluation of past performance as a guide for defining these areas. This is achieved through a process that involves diagnosing the existing situation, setting targets, and balancing the diagnosis with target-setting. The procedures to follow in this type of planning include defining the objectives for carrying out activities, defining the orientation which the system should take, and providing operational procedures to control the performance of the scientific and technological system in the selected domains of activity.

The objectives of activity planning are to provide priorities and general orientations for the activities performed by the scientific and technological system, and to propose measures to control and regulate the flow of knowledge originating abroad. The methodology should specify the type of activities to be given priority and the areas in which they should be concentrated, taking into account their possible contribution to economic and social development. Thus the tasks in activity planning can be divided into two groups: determination of the scientific and technological activities that should be carried out in the country, and specification of the areas in which scientific and technological knowledge will be acquired from foreign sources.

The philosophy underlying the category of activity planning is that scientific and technological autarky is practically impossible and even undesirable in the modern world, particularly for the underdeveloped countries of Latin America. The strategy proposed for scientific and technological development is one of selective interdependence with other countries and their scientific and technological systems. This implies that the underdeveloped country will seek to concentrate its scientific and technological efforts in areas for which it already has relatively high competence, or can acquire it in the short term, and in areas for which knowledge cannot (or should not) be imported. The local scientific community should attempt to transform itself into a world center for those particular areas of scientific and technological knowledge in which it has decided to concentrate its efforts, trying to compensate for the flow of imported knowledge. The selective interdependence strategy also implies the possibility that the country will import know-how, process it further, and then reexport it. Therefore, the selection of domains for scientific and technological activities becomes of crucial importance.

It is also necessary to control effectively the import of technology originating abroad, in order to ensure that in those areas in which the country will be dependent on foreign knowledge, it obtains the best possible conditions from its suppliers. The bitter experience of Latin American countries with regard to the acquisition of foreign technology shows the need for exerting more adequate control over the process of international transfers of technology to underdeveloped countries.

The methodology to be followed in determining domains and priorities for scientific and technological activities is based on the requirements and possibilities method,[15] which consists in comparing the capabilities or potential for science and technology with the demands or requirements of the economic, educational, physico-ecological, and other systems in the nation. It examines the functioning of these demand-generating systems, identifies their needs for knowledge, and brings them into the open. Once this is done, a comparison between requirements and possibilities is made to determine imbalances, seeking to couple demand for with supply of knowledge. This balancing process would replace the market mechanisms for scientific and technological knowledge which operate in countries with well-developed institutional structures.

However, it has been found necessary to modify and extend the approach proposed by this method, particularly by refining the general concept of requirements. In both the OECD and OAS versions of the method, requirements are derived from economic, educational, cultural, and other activities on the basis of a one-way analysis; the needs of demand-generating activities are projected into the scientific and technological system. The possibility that capabilities for science and technology may give rise to demand-generating activities, which in turn would create requirements for science and technology, is usually not considered. Figure 3.1 shows graphically the concepts to be introduced.

FIGURE 3.1

Types of Requirements for Science and Technology

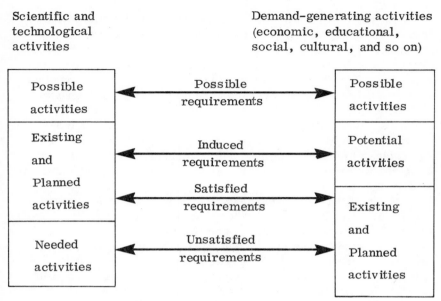

Source: Constructed by the author.

Each of the two groups of activities under consideration, the scientific and technological and the demand-generating groups, can be classified into several categories which could give rise to different types of requirements. Beginning with the demand-generating activities (economic, educational, social, cultural, and so on), there are existing and planned activities, which generate requirements for science and technology that may be satisfied or unsatisfied, depending on whether the relevant scientific and technological activities are being carried out or not. The unsatisfied requirements are those that generate a need for new scientific and technological activities, while the satisfied requirements find scientific and technological activities that correspond to the needs they create. Unsatisfied requirements may be identified at different levels. At an aggregate level, priorities for science and technology could be established for general problem areas of national importance, or for economic sectors. At the level of productive units and specific technologies, research projects could be identified and priorities attached to them. Different methods will have to be used for selecting areas of concentration and determining priorities at each of these levels.

On the other hand, there are existing scientific and technological activities that do not find counterparts in demand-generating activities. They could induce or promote economic, educational, social, and cultural activities that would in turn generate requirements for science and technology. Thus, scientific and technological activities in this category could create demand for themselves by promoting their corresponding economic, social, and other activities. Requirements derived from these induced demand-generating activities will be called induced requirements. The importance of induced requirements becomes apparent in the light of the characteristics of scientific and technological development in Latin America.

Many countries possess capabilities in some areas of fundamental, or even applied research, which have had little direct application. For example, it is not uncommon to find relatively high levels of competence in areas such as electronics, physics, and chemistry, for which there is no effective demand due to a lack of activity in the corresponding economic sectors. These capabilities for scientific and technological work could act as promoters or inducers of economic activities, which would in turn require the research services that the scientific and technological system is capable of providing. These induced requirements could play an important role, not only in the development of economic and social activities, but also in scientific and technological progress.

For the sake of completeness, it is possible to define another category of requirements for which neither the scientific and technological nor the demand-generating activities exist or are planned. These possible requirements would be generated by activities arising from a development strategy different from the one pursued by the country, and from a critical examination of the role that science and technology play in advancing economic growth under different models of development. This category of requirements becomes particularly important when the possibilities of skipping stages and of pursuing different styles of economic development are explicitly considered.

Therefore, at least four types of requirements can be identified: possible, induced, satisfied, and unsatisfied. The original version of the requirement and possibilities method, in both the OAS and OECD versions, considers only the last of these categories. Priorities for scientific and technological activities have been usually established from an analysis of existing and planned economic and social activities that generate unsatisfied requirements. The explicit consideration of possible and induced requirements would alter these priorities by taking into account potential and possible activities, and the demands for knowledge associated with them.

RESOURCE PLANNING

The last category, resource planning, deals with the allocation of resources, and it is conditioned by the availability of resources and by the possibility of directing the way in which they are allocated; it therefore puts emphasis on influencing the pattern of resource allocations to and within the system. Resource planning consists mainly of an allocative and distributive process, which should also allow the interpretation of allocation decisions within an experimental context. The procedures followed to carry out this type of planning activity include acquiring and distributing resources, defining specific aims and goals to be achieved with given resources, establishing priorities for resource allocation, and generating a data base which would allow the interpretation of each resource allocation decision, taking an experimental point of view, as a sample point in a universe of possible decisions.

Planning agencies seldom have under their control a sizable portion of the total resources allocated to science and technology; it is necessary to consider other institutions, such as private research organizations, universities, and government dependencies, as effectively engaged in resource planning, even if they are not conscious of the role they play. Taking the planning agency's point of view, resource planning should therefore be aimed at allocating its own resources efficiently, as well as at influencing the way in which other institutions and organizations in the scientific and technological system allocate their resources.

With regard to human resources, scientific and technology planning agencies in Latin America have little direct control over the preparation and training of highly qualified personnel. These are functions of universities and other institutes of higher education, and the agency in charge of planning scientific and technological development can only propose policies, coordinate efforts, and in general try to relate educational plans with scientific and technological development plans. Taking the areas of concentration defined in activity planning, the agency can point out to educational planners the needs for highly qualified researchers and technical personnel and suggest policies for retraining scientists whose skills appear to be irrelevant. It can also promote meetings and conferences to increase communication and interchange of experiences in the scientific community, as well as devise means for awarding prestige to scientific and technological activities that have direct relevance to development.

There are two areas of human resources planning in which the planning agency may exert control. These are the administration of fellowships and scholarships and the preparation of qualified personnel for scientific and technological planning and other supporting activities for the scientific and technological system. Through the administration of fellowships, particularly those to study abroad, the planning agency is in a position to influence directly the volume and composition of highly qualified personnel, and therefore, exert a certain degree of control in the orientation of its development. The preparation of personnel for science and technology planning and the training of all kinds of auxiliary personnel needed for supporting activities (documentation specialists and librarians, for example) are additional tasks which the planning agency can handle directly.

With regard to the allocation of financial resources, two different procedures may be followed, depending on whether funds are controlled directly by the planning agency or are under the control of other institutions. In the first case the resources made available to the planning agency should be allocated to the general areas defined in activity planning. If research activities in these areas can be performed directly by the planning agency or one of its dependencies the problem becomes one of generating and selecting the projects to which funds should be allocated. If projects are to be performed by other organizations, the planning agency should request that proposals be submitted in the domains or areas given priority. The problem then becomes one of selecting among research proposals submitted to the planning agency. Procedures such as cost/benefit analysis are available for this purpose. [16]

For the financial resources that are not directly under its control, the planning agency should propose allocation methods and ceiteria to other institutions, suggest uniform budgeting procedures which would allow interinstitutional comparisons, and initiate the preparation of an annual consolidated budget for science and technology, showing how financial resources are being allocated in the nation. Resource planning should also include the generation of information systems and a data base on resource allocation, which would help in the construction of mathematical models for the allocation of financial resources, and in the interpretation of allocation on decisions within an experimental framework.

Measures to rationalize the use of physical facilities should also be included in resource planning. These would refer to the use of buildings, laboratory equipment, instruments, computers, libraries, and documentation centers, among others. It is within the scope of the planning agency's functions to propose policies and plans that can lead to more efficient utilization of physical resources in the scientific and technological system.

The decisions involved in resource planning are in principle amenable to quantification, at least to a larger extent than those in activity, institutional, contextual, and stylistic planning, and the use of mathematical models may prove useful in this area. However, it is doubtful whether they are relevant at the stage of scientific and technological development in which most underdeveloped countries in Latin America are at present.

NOTES

1. Eric L. Trist, "The Relation of Welfare and Development in the Transition to Post-industrialism." Mimeographed. 1968.

2. James D. Caroll, "Participative Technology," Science 81 (1971): 647-53.

3. Russell L. Ackoff, A Concept of Corporate Planning (New York: Wiley, 1970).

4. Hasan Ozbekhan, "Toward a General Theory of Planning," in Perspectives of Planning (Paris: OECD, 1969).

5. On the methodology of scenarios see Pierre Andre Julien, Pierre Lamarde, and Daniel Latorche, La méthode des scenarios (Ottawa: Ministère d'état des sciences et technologie, November, 1971).

6. Piotr A. Kropotkin, Selected Writings on Anarchism and Revolution (Cambridge, Mass.: MIT Press, 1970), p. 47.

7. Ackoff, op. cit.

8. Ozbekhan, op. cit.

9. Bertram Gross, "Planning the Improbable," in Action Under Planning, ed. Bertram Gross (New York: McGraw Hill, 1967), p. 195.

10. Eric L. Trist, Appraising Administrative Capabilities for Development (New York: United Nations, 1969), p. 44.

11. René Maheu, National Science Policies in Countries of South and Southeast Asia (Paris: UNESCO, 1965), p. 10.

12. William F. Whyte, "Innovation or Imitation: Reflections on the Institutional Development of Peru," Administrative Science Quarterly 13 (1968): 371.

13. See Ackoff, op. cit.

14. See Chapter 7 of Francisco R. Sagasti, "Towards a Methodology for Planning Science and Technology in Underdeveloped Countries," Ph.D. Dissertation, University of Pennsylvania, 1972.

15. See Francisco Sagasti, Notes on the OECD and OAS Methods for Determining Requirements for Science and Technology (Washington, D.C.: Department of Scientific Affairs, OAS, 1971).

16. See Alberto Araoz and Mario Kamenetzky, Proyectos de inversión en ciencia y tecnología (Buenos Aires: Centro de Investigaciones en Administración Pública, 1975).

4

An Approach to Research
on Technology
Policy Implementation

THE EFFECTS OF POLICY AND CONTEXTUAL
FACTORS ON SCIENCE AND TECHNOLOGY:
AN OVERVIEW

One of the main concerns in technology policy research is to
analyze the effects of various influences on functions and activities
related to the production, diffusion, transfer, and utilization of
scientific and technological knowledge. This may be done for the
whole of the industrial sector (and other areas such as mining, infrastructure services, and so on, that may be of particular interest), and for certain branches of industry chosen for special study.
The analysis may start from the source of influence, looking at the
effects produced on the science and technology functions and activities, or, from a certain science and technology function or activity,
tracing back the sources of influence that produce effects on it.
The main idea is to explore cause-to-effect relationships in
an ordered way, generating partial explanatory hypotheses that,
once verified, may provide the basis for better control over science
and technology functions and activities so that they make a better
contribution to development objectives. Effects may be characterized by modifications in the orientation and magnitude of the dependent variables, or by constraints placed on such modifications. Such
cause-to-effect hypotheses will not usually be simple and unidirec-
tional, and many provisos will have to be incorporated in their

Used with permission from the monograph titled Methodological
Guidelines for the Science and Technology Policy Instruments (STPI)
Project, prepared with Alberto Araoz and revised after comments
from the country teams coordinator of the STPI project. First published by the International Development Research Centre of Canada
in 1976.

formulation; moreover, it may not be easy to express them in quantitative terms.

For analytical purposes it is possible to distinguish three groups of independent variables or types of influences:

Explicit science and technology policy and instruments. Here there exists a definite, identifiable purpose of causing an effect on science and technology functions and activities.

Implicit science and technology policy and instruments. Here the purpose is to produce effects on variables that do not belong to the group of science and technology functions and activities, but as a result, unintended effects happen to the latter. Such unintended effects may be termed side effects or implications. A better knowledge of them may enable policy makers to minimize or eliminate their negative influence or to heighten their positive effects, and eventually to transform these implicit policies and their related instruments into purposeful indirect policies and instruments for science and technology.

Contextual factors. These are factors that cannot be ascribed to current or recent government policies; they are a consequence of the country's past history, cultural and social features, resources, geography, and so on, and they are modifiable only in the long run. Their effect on science and technology functions and activities is principally to limit the impact of explicit or implicit policies and instruments. They may refer to broad macroeconomic, cultural, or social aspects, as well as to the characteristics of enterprises, research institutes, and the like, that are the result of the country's evolution.

Explicit and implicit science and technology policies and instruments may act directly on the dependent variables, but usually they do so through various institutions in charge of wielding them. The institutional setting may modify or distort the messages they transmit, thus affecting the magnitude of the resulting effect upon the dependent variable and the effectiveness of the instrument. Contextual factors also clearly influence the institutional setting and the way it works.

The dependent variables in the exercise are those functions and activities having to do with the production, diffusion, transfer, and utilization of science and technology. For analytical purposes they can be divided into three groups: those on the demand side, related to the technological behavior and the technological decisions of productive units; those on the supply side, related to the activities in the science and technology system proper that have as end products new technological knowledge and various scientific and technological

services; and those in what may be termed the linkage area, linking
the productive system with domestic and foreign sources of science
and technology knowledge.

SCIENCE AND TECHNOLOGY FUNCTIONS AND
ACTIVITIES (DEPENDENT VARIABLES)

The classification of science and technology functions and activities into demand, supply, and linkage groups comes naturally
from considering that scientific and technical knowledge is an important input for the production of goods and services and that productive units generate a demand for scientific and technical knowledge that is satisfied from local or foreign sources (demand side);
that there is domestic production of scientific and technological
knowledge, some of which feeds into productive units (supply side);
and that the flow of scientific and technical knowledge between the
producers and the users of such knowledge takes place through in-
termediary structures and institutions (linkage area). Instruments
for science and technology policy should act upon the functions and
activities of these three areas to achieve stated objectives.

The diagram in Figure 4.1 may be taken to represent the general situation in a country for all productive units and scientific activities, but a similar sketch may be made for industry and agriculture, or for specific industrial branches. In this case there would
be special interest in science and technology policy problems for the
branch in question: the vertex "productive units" would comprise
all those in the branch; the vertex "activities of the scientific and
technical system" would take into account those directly relevant to
the productive units of the branch, and their future development (one
may also include in this vertex other scientific activities that support the former ones); the activities in the linkage area would be
those that have to do with connecting the productive units of the
branch and the activities of the scientific and technical system, as
well as sources of foreign technology relevant to it. Some government policies affecting the production, diffusion, transfer, and
utilization of knowledge in the branch may be of an industry-wide
nature, whereas others may be specific to it.

An attempt should be made to deal with this complex network
of interactions whose elements are policies, science and technology
variables, effects on end variables, policy instruments, and so on,
without introducing excessively simplifying assumptions. The idea
is to systematize these interactions, maintaining a reasonable degree of complexity that will render useful research results. For
research purposes, an attempt should be made to list dependent

FIGURE 4.1

Science and Technology Functions and Activities
(dependent variables)

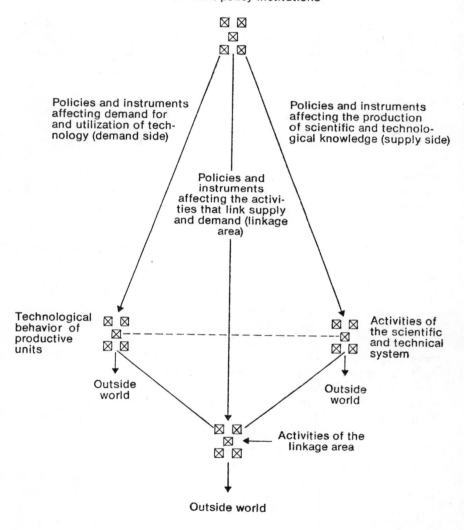

Source: Constructed by the author.

variables in each of the three main areas, in order to study causal chains from policy to effect and put forth partial explanatory hypotheses useful to policy makers. However, to make a list of dependent variables within each of the three groupings is not a simple thing, and any a priori attempt at a coherent taxonomy is open to criticism.

Demand Side: Productive Units

Two groupings of major variables can be identified at the productive unit level: the introduction of new knowledge, expressed as the demand for technology, and the assimilation and improvement of existing technology, which may be called the absorption of technology.

The demand for technology refers to knowledge needed for new (for the enterprise) products and processes that may originate from domestic or foreign sources, and that may appear in disembodied form (proprietary and nonproprietary knowledge, including that supplied through human resources), or as embodied technology (principally equipment and capital goods). It may be fruitful to break down this heading according to the source of the technology demanded.

A demand for domestic technology may come from the firm itself (research and development activities), or from the purchase of research and development activities and their results from outside the firm. Another source is technology that exists elsewhere in the country and is made available through diffusion, not involving compensation. A demand for foreign technology may be for proprietary or nonproprietary technology from foreign firms and institutions, technical cooperation and assistance from foreign governments or international agencies, or the stock of freely available knowledge that can be tapped through the literature, personal contacts, and visits or training abroad.

To handle new knowledge and its incorporation into production, the productive unit will have to make a number of technological decisions. Some are clearly concerned with the choice of alternatives regarding the source of new knowledge, the source of equipment, and the use of such inputs. Others have to do with the building up of the firm's capacity (technical and design groups, administrative organization, information) to make such choices, to adapt foreign technology (a very important activity because of the contribution it makes toward the optimal use of foreign technology and of the way it can link foreign technology to domestic scientific and technological activities), and to incorporate effectively new knowledge into production. The attitudes of decision makers toward technological innovation constitute an important ingredient in the way decisions are made.

The absorption of technology concerns activities directed toward the assimilation and improvement of technology that the productive unit has already incorporated, and comprises items such as production research, plan optimization, product development, the search for minor innovations, the adoption of quality control standards, trouble shooting, and other such technical activities within the firm; the purchase of scientific and technological services directly linked to productive activities that may come from the scientific and technological system or from foreign sources; and information about practices in other firms obtained through the diffusion process.

Supply Side

On the supply side the outcome is the supply of scientific and technological knowledge relevant to the productive system. Behind it may be distinguished three groups of functions and activities.

The generation of technology refers to the production or adaptation of scientific and technological knowledge to be incorporated in productive activities. There are a number of parameters and decisions affecting these functions and activities, such as number and characteristics of research centers, quality of the research and staff, orientation of their activities, and so on, and it is upon these that a study of the influence of policy instruments should be focused.

The supply of science and technology services similarly allows the productive system to use more efficiently the knowledge generated by the local science and technology system or purchased from foreign sources. These services also refer to the activities that allow the production of knowledge to proceed more efficiently.

The supply of scientific and technological skills focuses attention on the set of activities that supply human resources with the skills needed to carry out the whole range of science and technology functions and activities. This requires going beyond the general training given by the traditional educational system. Examples include the activities of graduate schools in science and engineering, various training programs for researchers, and continuing education schemes for engineers. Such activities are of great importance if science and technology are to be promoted effectively and put at the service of national objectives.

Linkage Area

The resulting variable, or outcome, in the linkage area is the facilitation and regulation of the transmission of scientific and technological knowledge to productive units. These are the functions and activities that relate the supply side to the demand side, and as such provide the channels through which technical knowledge can flow toward productive activities. On the other hand, they also channel the demands of the productive system to the local or foreign sources of knowledge. The activities related to such variables are those of extension services, engineering firms, organizations for control of technology imports, industrial information systems, and the like.

SOURCES OF INFLUENCE (INDEPENDENT VARIABLES)

Each of the three types of sources of influence considered will be examined in turn, although more attention is given to explicit policies and their corresponding instruments, since many of the concepts that refer to them will be used in the examination of other sources of influence.

Explicit Science and Technology Policy and Its Instruments

Explicit science and technology policy and its instruments refers to policies and instruments that have a definite and explicit purpose to provoke an effect on science and technology functions and activities. The purpose originates in a policy expressed in documents or statements of varying degrees of normative power. A policy may sometimes directly affect the dependent variable it is designed to influence, but more often it needs an instrument that acts through an organizational structure and a set of operational mechanisms.

The Concept of Policy Instruments

An explicit science and technology policy is a statement by a high level government official or institution (such as a department or the planning agency) that deals with an issue in science and technology; it expresses a purpose (effects to be produced upon science and technology variables) and may set objectives, define desired outcomes, and establish quantitative goals. Policies also contain criteria for choosing among alternatives with regard to the performance of science and technology functions and activities, providing guidance for decision making. Although policies refer primarily to orientations set by government officials, they may also be formulated by representatives of the private sector. The issue dealt with may be very specific, referring to some particular purpose or decision to be taken and the criteria associated with it, or it may be of a general nature.

A policy may remain a mere rhetorical statement if no means are provided to implement and realize its potential effect. To avoid this a number of things may be needed, and they will be incorporated under the term policy instrument. A policy instrument constitutes the set of ways and means used when putting a given policy into practice. It can be considered as the vehicle through which those in charge of formulating and implementing policies actualize their capability to influence decisions taken by others.

A science and technology policy instrument is one in which the ways and means (or actualized capabilities) include as a significant component the manipulation of science and technology variables. Also, a policy instrument attempts to make individuals and institutions take decisions following the rationality dictated by the collective objectives established by those in power. It is the connecting link between the purpose expressed in a policy and the effect that is sought in practice. A policy instrument is called direct when it refers explicitly to science and technology functions and activities, and indirect when, although referring primarily to policies, functions, or activities other than science and technology, it has an important indirect effect on science and technology functions and activities.

An instrument is a complex entity taken here to comprise one or more of the following items:

A legal device,* which may also be called the "legal instrument." This embodies the policy, or parts of it in the form of a law, decree, or regulation. Formal agreements and contracts may also be considered in this category. The important thing is that a legal device goes one step beyond a policy by stipulating obligations, rights, rewards, and penalties connected with its being obeyed.

An organizational structure, that is put in charge of implementing the policy. The term organizational structure may include one or more institutions; that is, a policy may be implemented through one or more existing institutions, or a new one may come

---

*The words "legal device" are used as a translation of the Spanish "dispositivo legal" or "disposición legal," which refers to any legal or formalized agreement that carries prescriptive weight, is imposed by some authority, and is sanctioned in some way by the society within which it is issued.

into being. This may be thought of as the "hardware" aspect of the organizational structure. The term may also include the procedures, methodologies, decision criteria, and programs that may span one or more institutions. These are of an administrative and technical nature, and specify the steps that must be carried out in processing or combining pertinent information for the purpose of applying the policy. They may be considered as the "software" aspect of the organizational structure. Often, science and technology policies are implemented through organizational structures that already exist for other policy areas. For instance, a law allowing the free import of scientific equipment would naturally be implemented through existing import control mechanisms and institutions.

A set of operational mechanisms, which are the levers, or actual means, through which the organizational structure finally implements the decisions on a day-to-day basis, and attempts to obtain the desired effect on the variables the policy has set out to influence.

Throughout the analysis of an instrument it is important to keep in mind the "actors" or key decision makers who are directly involved in the design and use of a policy instrument. An instrument does not act on its own, and responds to the will of the policy makers and decision makers using it. More will be said about this later. The conceptualization of policy instrument can be seen in Figure 4.2, although there may be cases where some of the component elements of a policy instrument are missing.

More complex situations may be represented using the concepts outlined, such as the two cases in Figure 4.3. In (a) are found a number of instruments that intend to provoke different effects on account of one (complex) policy statement on one or more issues, such as a development plan. This may be called a policy-oriented cluster of instruments. In (b) various instruments, which obey several policies, all have effects on one variable. This may be called a function-oriented cluster of instruments.

Description of an Instrument

Using the concepts and diagrams set forth previously, it is possible to describe and analyze a diversity of science and technology policies and instruments. Such description should pay attention to the policy level at which the instrument originates and the type of science and technology function or activity it attempts to influence.

Instruments may be classified according to whether the policy/instrument couple affects the demand side, the supply side, or the linkage area. This may be crossed with two categories according to the policy level--that is, whether the policy originates in a government body that has a broad policy mandate, or in a particular

FIGURE 4.2

Structure of a Policy Instrument

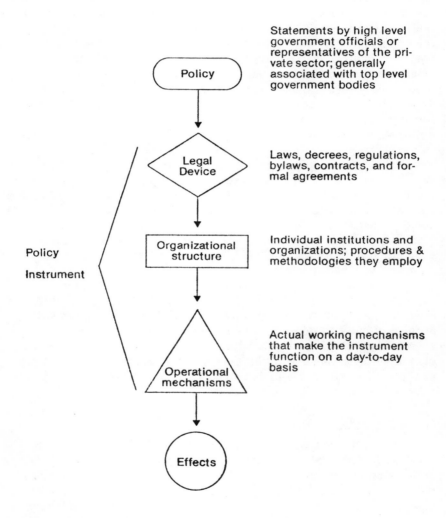

Source: Constructed by the author.

FIGURE 4.3

Cluster of Instruments

(a)

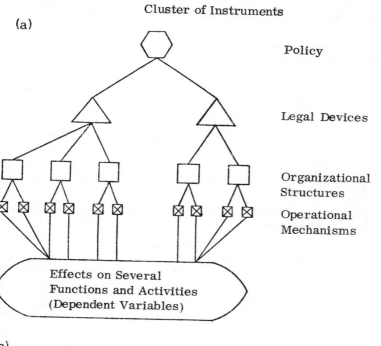

Policy

Legal Devices

Organizational
Structures

Operational
Mechanisms

Effects on Several
Functions and Activities
(Dependent Variables)

(b)

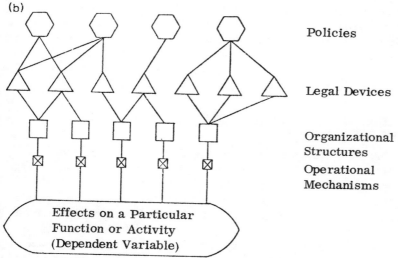

Policies

Legal Devices

Organizational
Structures

Operational
Mechanisms

Effects on a Particular
Function or Activity
(Dependent Variable)

Note: (a) Policy-oriented cluster of instruments; (b) function-
oriented cluster of instruments.
Source: Constructed by the author.

organization at a lower level (that may not even belong to the government, such as a producers' association, a large private enterprise, or a research institute). The distinction between these two levels may be useful when identifying the main policy instruments that act on a branch of industry or on the whole industrial sector. Table 4.1 shows this two-way classification with some examples.

Other criteria for classifying instruments include their discretionary or nondiscretionary character. The former involves a decision by some administrative authority in the application of an instrument, while in the latter, application follows automatically from a definite rule without the possibility of discrimination. Discretionary instruments require the existence of an administrative capability and allow focusing on individual productive units, research institutes, and the like in the implementation of policies. On the other hand, they give the opportunity for interference arising in their application (bribes, arbitrariness, and so on). Nondiscretionary instruments affect science and technology functions across the board, without allowing distinctions according to the particular situations of the different entities affected by the policy and the instrument. They require a simpler organizational and administrative infrastructure for their application, and reduce the possibility of interference by interested parties.

It is possible to enlarge the set of criteria by which to classify policy instruments, by including categories such as positive or negative instruments, depending on whether they are aimed at stimulating, encouraging, facilitating, and inducing, or whether they impose restrictions, prevent actions from being taken, prohibit certain activities, and so on. However, the set of categories proposed above should provide a sufficient basis for the classification of S and T policy instruments.

The Operation of a Policy Instrument and the Role of the Policy Keepers

The concepts advanced up to now do not take into account the dynamics and changing characteristics of policy instruments and the intervention of those who wield them. In practice a policy instrument does not remain fixed and immutable, but evolves through a series of stages before it is made obsolete and replaced by another policy instrument. In this process of growth, maturation, and decay of policy instruments, the agents in charge of operating them, who may be called the policy keepers, play a most important role.

The genesis of a policy instrument spans a period that begins with the formulation of the policy itself. At this stage the policy maker plays the most important role and it is his responsibility to steer the formulation of a policy up to the point where the instruments

TABLE 4.1

Classification for Explicit Science and Technology Policy

Policy Level	Science and Technology Functions and Activities Affected		
	Demand side: technological behavior and decisions in productive system	Supply side: activities in the science and technology system	Linkage area: activities that link productive system with sources of science and technology
High (emanating from an institution with a broad policy mandate)	For example, articles or sections in general laws, industrial promotion laws, development plans	For example, science policy statements, for instance, on the budget for R & D	For example, policies and legislation on technology transfer, technical co-operation agreements with other nations
Low (emanating from an individual institution without broad mandate)	For example, policies and decisions of development banks, state enterprises, and government agencies	For example, decisions about government R & D contracts and grants	For example, decisions made by agencies in charge of regulating technology transfer and technical cooperation

Source: Compiled by the author.

for its implementation are designed and approved. The life of a policy instrument begins when the legal devices, organizational structures, and operational mechanisms necessary for its functioning are established.

The dynamics of policy implementation will force the introduction of many changes in one or more of the components of the instruments. Modifications of the initial laws and decrees must be enacted, organizations will have to be modified, operational procedures changes, and, in general, the instrument will undergo a process of mutation through subsequent modifications so as to make it more appropriate for the purposes of implementing the policies under consideration. These processes of mutation and change take place through the active intervention of those in charge of operating the instrument--the policy keepers. In a sense it can be said that the policy keeper is a part of the operational mechanism of the instrument, given the fact that he operates within the framework provided by the legal devices and the organizational structures, and that he is in charge of the day-to-day operation of the policy instrument. Nevertheless, this should not obscure the fact that he is also capable of modifying the legal and organizational framework within which he operates.

The policy keeper thus emerges as the key agent who has the task of keeping the instrument functioning in accordance with the original criteria established in the policy, and to this end he must devise and introduce the modifications that are necessary in its structure. From these remarks it is clear that the scope for action of a policy keeper will be much greater when dealing with discretionary instruments. It is also clear that in many circumstances the distinction between the policy maker and the policy keeper may be artificial, and that the responsibility of designing and operating the policy instrument can fall on the same person.

In practice, the policy keeper for a particular instrument may comprise more than one individual (for example a committee) and may handle several other policy instruments at the same time. A combination of a few policy makers and policy keepers may have control over a cluster of policy instruments, carrying out their activities through a network of formal and informal contact and providing support to each other as the need arises. The network of informal contacts of policy keepers is particularly important, for the actual performance and impact of policy instruments may depend more on these contacts than on the formal procedures established in the legal device, the institutional structures, and the operational mechanisms.

Evaluation of the Performance
of Policy Instruments

The assessment of the performance of an instrument of science and technology policy is rather difficult, but an attempt should be made to characterize policy instruments, or clusters of instruments, according to their usefulness in implementing certain policies. This raises several complex questions: Should an instrument be evaluated independently of the policy with which it is associated? Is there a group of instruments better suited to a set of policies, purposes, or strategies than others? Is there an absolute measure of the effectiveness of an instrument, or should an attempt be made to carry out comparative analyses? How should the performance of policy keepers be evaluated? However, there are a few concepts and tentative definitions that may provide some guidance in this evaluation. Ultimately, the decision to use one instrument or another in the implementation of science and technology policies should depend on some evaluation of its characteristics along the lines suggested below.

The scope and specificity of an instrument refer to the range of science and technology functions and activities it affects, or the types of technological decisions it can influence. This attribute of an instrument could also refer to the size and volume of the functions and activities it affects; the larger the number of science and technology functions and activities an instrument affects, the wider its scope. On the other hand, it would be a very specific instrument if designed to affect one particular science and technology function focusing on some predetermined group of enterprises, agencies, or research institutions.

The coverage of an instrument can be defined as the absolute number or proportion of productive units, government agencies, research organizations, and so on that the instrument is capable of affecting. This concept may be extended to include side effects and implications. The equity of an instrument refers to the equality of its impact on all units that have similar characteristics. Diverse situations, exceptions, and loopholes may give rise to a situation in which the instrument cannot be applied with fairness in all cases that have similar characteristics.

The efficiency of an instrument indicates the relation between the effort put forth (administrative, financial, technical) and the effects that result from its use. The effort may include considerations of a quantitative character, such as cost involved in its application, or of a qualitative character, such as expertise needed to operate it.

Other parameters to evaluate the performance of policy instruments may include the time lags involved in its application, the flexibility with which it can be used (meaning the possibility of applying it or not, according to the circumstances), the amount of information required for its application (meaning the degree to which it preserves its properties in the light of contextual changes), and other parameters of similar nature. Of particular importance is the concept of <u>effectiveness</u> of an instrument, which refers to the likelihood of obtaining the desired result; that is, implementing the policy, and affecting the behavior of productive units, units in the science and technology system, and units in the linkage area. However, this may be a rather difficult proposition, because instruments do not function in a simple, linear way, and there exist side effects that complicate the assessment of an instrument's effectiveness. This emphasizes the necessity to take into account the effect of the instrument, not only on the functions and activities it is specifically designed to influence, but also on other variables and on the effectiveness of other instruments as well.

Another problem that arises in the evaluation of the effectiveness of an instrument is that often it is designed to influence more than one science and technology function and may achieve this with varying degrees of success. Therefore, it may be necessary to examine the effectiveness of an instrument as a whole, considering the several science and technology functions it should affect, and even the side effects it has on functions and activities in fields other than science and technology.

Throughout the discussion on performance "instrument" has been used in the singular, but the concepts may also be applied to a cluster of instruments. Also, it is necessary to take into account explicitly the fact that the performance of an instrument depends on the skills and ability of the policy keepers in charge of its operation.

Implicit Science and Technology Policy and Its Instruments

Many policies and decisions aimed at functions and activities other than science and technology may have unintended effects upon the latter. These effects are seldom taken into account in the design of policies and policy instruments, and policy makers have, at best, a dim awareness of them. It is useful to consider two types of unintended effects, differentiated according to whether the effects are potential or actually take place. The first may be called implications, and the second, side effects. Implications refer to what may happen to science and technology functions and activities as a result of new policies and decisions in other areas, and the testing of any hypotheses about them would require relying on opinions and other nonfactual evidence. Hence, any verification of hypotheses about implications would be weak. Side effects refer to what has actually happened, so that actual behavior may be studied, giving a strong verification based on factual data. Of course it is not easy to draw a line between the two types of unintended effects, and in some cases the study of side effects may rely on abundant empirical evidence, while in others only bits and pieces may be found.

A wide array of policies may have side effects and implications for science and technology variables. For example, high level policies include articles or sections of general laws (such as agriculture, land reform, health, mining), industrial promotion laws, general and sectoral development plans, international agreements (particularly in commercial matters), budgetary decisions at the national level, decisions about wages and social security, and so on. Low level policies and decisions include the credit system, foreign exchange regulations, characteristics of investment decisions, foreign trade decisions (particularly about import permits and import tariffs), manipulation of operative controls for the regulation of industry, and so on; purchasing decisions by state enterprises, purchasing decisions by large private enterprises (in particular foreign-owned ones), and in general, decisions by government agencies with some autonomy in their behavior that may strongly affect science and technology functions and activities. The checklist in Table 4.2 identifies policies in other areas that may have an important impact on science and technology. Some of the items may also be included in the category of contextual factors.

The study of the effects of implicit policies may follow a pattern similar to that of the explicit science and technology policies and instruments. The sequence--policy, legal device, organizational structure, operational mechanism--can be described in each case.

An analysis of the science and technology policies implicit in general laws (on industrialization, mining, foreign investment, and so on) should uncover the main implications or side effects for science and technology functions and activities. The first step should be to identify those policies oriented to areas other than S and T that could have an important impact on them. For this there is a need for a certain understanding of the way the science and technology system functions in the country, through an examination of its place in relation to the economic, social, and educational systems.

Once the set of policies with potential effects on S and T functions and activities has been identified and ordered according to their likely degree of influence on science and technology, it is possible to proceed with a detailed analysis of each. Although the form and content of laws will vary a great deal from country to country, it is

TABLE 4.2

Implicit Science and Technology Policies Indirectly Affecting Scientific and Technological Activities

(a) Economic (primarily directed to the functioning of the economic system)
--finance (credit, interest rates)
--fiscal (taxation, exchange rates, exchange control)
--external trade (tariff and nontariff barriers)
--internal trade (prices, marketing, government procurement)
--wages and labor compensation policies
--foreign investment, compensation, and nationalization
--economic development policies
--specific industrial policies
--specific agricultural policies
--legal and general instruments
--policies toward regional development

(b) Manpower
--educational system (literacy, primary, secondary, vocational, etc. education)
--higher education policies (universities, training, institutes, management training, post-doctoral training)
--fellowship policies
--industrial training and retraining, technician training
--policies for the use of foreign manpower
--policies toward emigration of professionals
--policies toward repatriation of skilled manpower
--policies related to mobility of qualified personnel
--policies for the promotion of human resources
--salary structure and awards; mobility

(c) Cultural
--mechanisms to modify the general value structures, attitudes, norms, etc., including the position of women
--policies toward modernization and technological change
--popularization of science and technology
--policies toward modifying the structure of status and prestige awarding procedures, mechanisms, etc.

(d) Physico-ecologic
--policies for the exploitation and preservation of natural resources
--policies toward environmental control, pollution

(e) Demographic and social
--health care
--mortality rates
--population control
--income policies, distribution of income
--policies toward increasing social mobility

Source: Compiled by the author.

possible to suggest a general outline for extracting the implicit science and technology policies.

The first task would be to focus on the articles and clauses that could affect science and technology functions in enterprises, government agencies, research organizations, universities, and so on, describing their possible effect. The second stage would be to put together the implications of different clauses and articles referring to a single issue or S and T function, assessing their effect by taking them as a whole. These potential effects or implications could then be put together across a single law or several of them, and also across various science and technology functions and activities, to identify the overall implicit policy.

When examining the implicit policies contained in general laws, one of three situations may arise regarding the content of the implicit policy uncovered:

The implications of the policy are so obvious and clearly defined that a conclusion may be arrived at as a result of the analysis.

The implications of the policy for science and technology functions and activities are not so clear and obvious, and their definite impact will depend on reactions of the enterprises, government agencies, research institutes, and so on. The specific and actual content of implicit policy will have to be determined through empirical analyses, and the most that can be done is to formulate hypotheses on the effect of the law being analyzed.

The law leads to the identification of instances of intervention by government agencies, and the content of implicit policy will depend on the way decisions are made by government officials (the policy keepers). To uncover the implicit content of science and technology policy, an analysis of such decisions is in order.

Note that the discussion is about implications, although it is clear that if empirical data were available to corroborate the statements spelled out in the implicit policy, they would be referred to as side effects.

A similar procedure could be followed with regard to development plans. In this case it would be possible to make a direct comparison of implicit and explicit policies arising out of a single document. A plan generally contains clearly spelled-out objectives, policies, and strategies, as in the case of general development plans, industrial development plans, manpower plans, and so on. The procedure in this case could be as follows. First, summarize the main objectives, policies, and strategic elements of the plan, examining each of them with regard to their impact on science and technology functions and activities. Second, deduce what would be required in terms of science and technology functions and activities in order to be able to fulfill the objectives stated, to comply with the policies, or to follow the strategy. This would lead to an identification of the prerequisites, from the point of view of science and technology, that are necessary to carry out the plan. The whole set of prerequisites would constitute the implicit science and technology policy contained in the plan. Third, summarize the components of the plan referring explicitly to science and technology, putting them in terms of the science and technology functions and activities defined in the research. Fourth, compare the implicit and explicit components of science and technology policy in the plan, examining their coherence and the correspondence between the two. A plan, by definition, consists of statements about what is to be done and therefore, unless past performance is being compared with planned objectives, it is possible only to derive implications and not side effects from such an analysis.

If the study of implicit policies were focusing on speeches, white papers, specific legal regulations, or other sources of implicit policies, a different treatment would be required. These two cases, general laws and development plans, may provide an orientation of the research procedures that may be followed. The uncovering of implicit policies that significantly affect science and technology functions and activities would also lead to identifying the policy instruments associated with them that could be used as indirect instruments to implement science and technology policies.

Contextual factors

There are aspects of the social system that cannot be changed in the short run, in contrast to policies that in principle may be rapidly modified. It is suggested, as an operational line of demarcation, that if a certain characteristic cannot be changed significantly during a plan period of, say, four or five years, it should be considered a contextual factor. The contextual factors of interest here are those that a priori appear to have some effects on scientific and technological functions and activities, either directly or indirectly, through their influence on the organizational structure in implementing policies. The effects can take the shape of constraints and limitations on what an explicit scientific and technological policy may attempt to do or achieve, or they may imply drawbacks and obstacles to the way the organizational structures function, thus having an influence on the effectiveness of instruments.

Three different types of contextual factors can be identified: invariant contextual factors, referring primarily to the country's physical and geographical characteristics (resource endowment, climate, size, location), which cannot be changed except by cataclysmic events; superstructural contextual factors, referring to the sociocultural structure of the country, which in principle are amenable to change in the long run, but might be compressed into a shorter period through revolutionary upheaval (cultural traits, value norms, relations of production, and so on); and contextual factors resulting from long-term cumulative policy making, referring to some of the characteristics of the economic system resulting from policies implemented in a piecemeal fashion over a long span of time. Examples would be the characteristics of the industrial structure arising out of pursuing import substituting policies, and the behavior and attitudes of entrepreneurs resulting from an artificially easy environment for their activities, and so on. The concept of contextual factors may be further subdivided according to whether they influence the total economy, or whether they act primarily at the sectoral level.

Many contextual factors carry a negative connotation typical of underdevelopment, and one of the aims of a development process is to change them in the long run. For example, it is possible to point out the lack of pressures to perform science and technology functions and activities in underdeveloped countries, arising out of contextual factors that result from the structure of the economy and from cumulative policy making over several decades. Among the contextual factors that limit and condition the effect of explicit science and technology policy and instruments are the size of the national economy, dependence on a few export items, unavailability of a wide range of efficient technological alternatives, chronic inflation, heavy reliance on foreign technology, land tenure patterns, small size of many enterprises, oligopolistic and monopolistic structures, unfavorable salary structures and characteristics of labor legislation, deficient communications and information systems, deformed price formation mechanisms, high unemployment, predominance of foreign investment in certain sectors of economic activity, and so on.

Other relevant contextual factors may be briefly mentioned:

Cultural: habits of cultural dependence; ties of scientists to the international network of science; unfavorable value structures, attitudes, norms, and so on, such as disdain for manual labor, humanistic and antiscientific traditions, attitudes toward women's labor; structure of status and prestige.

Social and demographic: low educational levels, internal and external brain drain, deficiencies in the educational system, poor labor mobility, unavailability of skilled manpower, poor health, overpopulation, heavy rural-urban migration, structural unemployment and underemployment.

Political and institutional: poorly defined national development objectives; lack of awareness of the potential role of science and technology in development; habitual lack of coordination between policies emanating from various high- and low-level sources; heavy-handed and slow decision-making procedures; excessive red tape; slow and complex control of expenditures; corruption; poor control of the implementation of government policies and decisions; fossilized institutions and mechanisms that subsist long after they stop being useful; inefficiency of public administration.

Geographical, physical, and ecological: lack of certain natural resources; poor transport and communications within and without the country; ecological problems; climatic factors. It is clear that in each case it becomes necessary to identify which contextual factors are of relevance to the formulation and implementation of science and technology policies.

APPROACHES TO RESEARCH ON TECHNOLOGY
POLICY IMPLEMENTATION

There are in principle two approaches to the study of science and technology policy implementation. One starts from policies, tracing down their effects--the top-down approach--and the other starts from the effects, tracing back the sources of influence behind them--the bottom-up approach. The two approaches are complementary. The first is useful for examining the effects of existing or intended policies (legislation, development plans, and practices of government agencies), and if a screening of key policies (explicit and implicit) is done for a particular branch, or even for the whole industrial sector, a resultant policy may be derived. This policy would express the combined effects of the key policies on science and technology variables, acting through the existing institutional setting and within the constraints imposed by the relevant contextual factors.

The second approach seeks to answer more specific questions about the sources of influence acting on a single issue, variable, or problem area of science and technology functions and activities. For instance, one may be interested in why state enterprises in the metallurgical industries buy their capital equipment predominantly from foreign sources; or why the whole of the modern industrial sector tends to use capital-intensive technologies. The bottom-up approach would lead to the identification of significant influences, both external (policies, instruments, and context) and internal (technical capacity, information available, decision patterns, influence of decisions that do not strictly refer to science and technology matters), on the productive unit. This knowledge would help to improve the situation by modifying existing policies, introducing new policies, removing constraints, generating new instruments, and so on. Such an analysis would also give a good idea of the degree of congruence of the various policy instruments and decisions emanating from different sources--what has been called here the function-oriented cluster of instrument--and hence about the resulting effect of this cluster on the variable under study.

The examples above have referred to the demand side of science and technology--that is, what takes place in productive units--but similar examples could also be given in regard to units on the supply side and in the linkage area.

To avoid spreading efforts too thinly, research efforts should focus on a few important policies and their instruments and on a few issues related to science and technology functions and activities. This implies choosing a few branches of industry in each country, but it may be necessary to restrict the domain of inquiry even further. The sequence of research under either of the two approaches should be identification of presumed cause-to-effect links; formulation of hypotheses about the effect of policy variables (explicit or implicit) on dependent science and technology variables, as well as hypotheses about the effectiveness of explicit science and technology policy instruments; and verification (weak or strong, as the case may be) of such hypotheses.

In some cases it may be enough to consider the interactions between sources of influence and science and technology variables, without introducing into the analysis the internal characteristics of the decision unit (productive unit, unit in supply of technology, unit in the linkage area) whose output is being studied. This is tantamount to considering the unit as a "black box" that receives an input--the policy acting through an instrument within the constraints of the relevant contextual factors--and produces an output, namely, changes in the science and technology variable under study (see Figure 4.4). This may be a useful simplification when the researcher is interested in the aggregate effect of the policy variable on many decision units taken together, and when these units are not too large and have similar characteristics, so that a certain degree of homogeneity may be assumed. However, when dealing with large units whose particular behavior is of special interest, or those in a monopolistic or predominant situation in their branches or sectors (such as a large state enterprise in the oil and petrochemical field, or an agricultural research institute that handles a large share of

FIGURE 4.4

The Technology Decision Unit as a Black Box

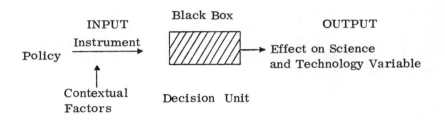

Source: Constructed by the author.

FIGURE 4.5

The Technology Decision Unit as a Partially Opened Black Box

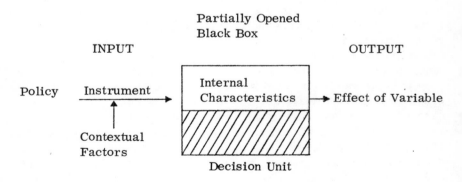

Source: Constructed by the author.

research in the agricultural sector), it is necessary also to look into what happens inside the unit. This requires an understanding of the internal characteristics that, together with the external influence of the policy variable(s), may allow a better explanation of the effect on the science and technology functions and activities under study. Hence the black box should be opened as much as necessary for the formulation of better, more powerful hypotheses (see Figure 4.5).

In the case of a productive unit, the internal characteristics of interest are those aspects of its "hardware" (physical and human resources and their organization) and "software" (procedures, methodologies, decision rules, motivations behind these) that are especially relevant to the way in which the unit makes the set of technological decisions that constitute its technological behavior. The main advantage of this opening of the black box is that it may give the researchers a better idea about which internal characteristics to modify, through other policies, to permit an existing or proposed explicit science and technology policy to obtain the desired effects.

A treatment parallel to what has been suggested in the case of productive units may be applied to units on the supply side and in the linkage area; those large units that dominate a sector or branch would need an analysis of the internal characteristics that condition their technological behavior.

5

Guidelines for Technology Policies

INTRODUCTION

During the past ten years a great deal of work has been carried out in Latin America on science and technology policy making
and planning. The efforts of researchers have spanned a wide
spectrum covering diagnosis of the existing situation, collection of
data on scientific and technological activities, formulation of conceptual models, and design of strategies and policies. As a result,
the Latin American countries have accumulated an experience
larger than that of other Third World countries, with the possible
exception of India. From these studies certain common issues begin to emerge and, although there are a few gaps in the knowledge
of the situation in science and technology, these basic characteristics and trends have been confirmed at one time or another in a
variety of situations and countries. For example, the studies on
licensing agreements as a means for technology transfer were initiated in the late 1960s in the Andean Pact, were extended to Argentina, Brazil, and Mexico, and are now being carried out in the
Central American countries. All have shown more or less the same
things (proliferation of restrictive clauses, existence of overpricing, concentration of suppliers, and so on). The studies on innovation at the enterprise level, on the scientific and technological
potential of Latin American countries, and on the diffusion of technical information, show a similar pattern.

Taking these studies into account, several countries and regional organizations have taken action on the formulation and implementation of science and technology policies. Thus, the Organization

Used with permission from a paper published in <u>Science and
Public Policy</u> 4 (January 1977): 2-15.

of American States (OAS) Pilot Project of Transfer of Technology, the actions taken by the Andean Pact through decisions 24, 84, 85, 86, and 89, the initiation of registries for technology transfer in Argentina and Brazil, and the creation of institutions such as Instituto de Investigación Tecnológica Industrial y de Normas Técnicas (ITINTEC) in Peru (or the modification of existing ones such as in the case of the Instituto Nacional de Technólogia Industrial (INTI in Argentina)—all show that there has been a move from diagnosis to implementation (see Chapters 6 and 7). The need to learn rapidly from these experiences in policy design and implementation has led to the organization of research efforts such as the Science and Technology Policy Instruments (STPI) project in six Latin American and four non-Latin American countries.[1]

Some general concepts of science and technology policy that have emerged as a result of the studies mentioned will be traced in this chapter, in particular those sponsored by the OAS, the Andean Pact, and those that were carried out by the STPI project research network under the sponsorship of the International Development Research Centre (IDRC) of Canada and the OAS. Taking a perspective derived from personal experience, this study will attempt to bridge the gap between diagnosis and conceptualization, on the one hand, and specific actions at the practical level, on the other, giving an indication of the types of policies and policy instruments that can be used to enhance the technological capabilities of industry in Latin American countries.

Before entering into the subject matter, it is necessary to draw a distinction between two concepts that are usually put together. The confusion between science policy and technology policy has been responsible for many mistakes with regard to enhancement of technical capabilities, particularly for industry. This chapter will deal exclusively with technology policy. One of the key errors in this field in Latin America has been that the habits of thought, concepts, ideas, criteria, and policy instruments that refer to science policy have been extended to deal with technology policy, even though the two have rather different characteristics and require different approaches. Table 5.1 summarizes the differences between science policy and technology policy at a national level.

Science policy deals with activities related primarily to scientific research. They produce basic and applied knowledge, which cannot be used directly in productive activities. There is little possibility of appropriating for economic purposes the results of scientific research, and ownership is assured primarily by widespread and open publication. The criteria for the evaluation of activities to be performed (research projects) are primarily internal to the scientific community and have little to do with specific national

TABLE 5.1

Differences between Science and Technology Policies at the National Level

	Science Policy	Technology Policy
Objectives	To generate scientific (basic and potentially useful) knowledge which may eventually feed into social and economic uses, and which will allow understanding and keeping up with the evolution of science; to develop a base of scientific activities and of human resources linked to the growth of knowledge at the world level	To acquire the technology and the technical capabilities for the production of goods and the provision of services; to develop the national capacity for autonomous decision making in matters of technology
Main type of activities covered	Basic and applied research, which generate basic knowledge and potentially useful knowledge	Development, adaptation, reverse engineering, technology transfer, and engineering, which generate ready-to-use knowledge
Appropriation of the results of activities covered	Results (in the form of basic and potentially useful knowledge) appropriated by disseminating them widely; ownership ensured by publishing	Results (in the form of ready-to-use knowledge) remaining largely in the hands of those who generated them; appropriation of results ensured by patents, secret know-how, and human-embodied knowledge
Reference criteria for the performance of activities	Primarily internal to the scientific community; evaluation of activities based mainly on scientific merit, and in a few cases on possible applications	Primarily external to the technical and engineering community; evaluation of activities based mainly on their contribution to social and economic objectives
Scope of activities	Universal; worldwide validity of activities and results	Localized (firm, branch, sector, or national level); activities and results valid in a specific context
Amenability to planning	Programming possible for only broad areas and directives; results dependent on the capacity of researchers (teams and individuals) to generate new ideas; large uncertainties associated	Stricter programming of activities and sequences possible; little new knowledge generally required; systematic use of existing knowledge involved; less uncertainty associated
Dominant time horizon	Long- and medium-term	Short- and medium-term

Source: Compiled by the author.

needs (although it is possible to trace from a specific socioeconomic need, through development and applied research activities, all the way back to scientific research).

On the other hand, activities covered by technology policy have as their main objective the acquisition of technology to be used in productive and social processes, as well as the development of a national capacity for autonomous decision making in matters of technology. The activities covered involve development work, adaptation of existing techniques, reverse engineering, technology transfer, production research, and other activities that produce or generate and enhance the stock of ready-to-use knowledge. The appropriation of results for economic purposes is a characteristic of the activities covered, and there are several mechanisms (such as the patent system) to make possible this appropriation. In addition, the economic use of this knowledge is guaranteed by secrecy, by the fact that most of the knowledge generated is human-embodied, and that it is subject to various degrees of monopolistic appropriation.

There are also several differences arising out of the types of institutions that have dealt (and are dealing) with science policy and with technology policy. There is a marked emphasis on educational institutions in the case of the former, and a predominance of industrialization agencies in charge of the latter. Also, the manpower requirements (in terms of quantity and type of training), and the types of information needed, make it necessary to distinguish between science and technology policies, particularly when moving from the conceptual to the operational level.

PRINCIPLES FOR TECHNOLOGY POLICY*

On the basis of the knowledge and experience accumulated to date, it is possible to identify several principles on which the development of sound and coherent technology policies should be based. These principles represent the minimum common denominator that must be agreed on, if the subject of technology policy is to be treated seriously.

First, technological progress—defined as the continuous and cumulative process of creation, diffusion, and utilization of knowledge—is one of the most important factors in the socioeconomic

---

*This and the following sections are based partially on Chapter 2 in Francisco Sagasti and Mauricio Guerrero, El Desarrollo Científico y Tecnológico de América Latina (Buenos Aires: BID/INTAL, 1974).

development of Latin America. In order to overcome the situation of underdevelopment, Latin American countries must counteract the negative effects of the technological domination exercised by the industrialized nations and their large enterprises. This will be achieved only by simultaneously attending to the creation of an indigenous technological capacity and to the regulation of the process of importation of foreign technology, and by promoting the demand for local technology.

Second, the importance acquired by science and technology in the development process makes it necessary to establish an explicit and coherent technology policy, differentiated from science, economic, labor, educational, and industrial policies, although closely related to them. The technology policy must be subordinated to economic and social development; technological progress cannot be considered an end by itself, but a means toward attaining broader objectives. The growing complexity of the development process generates a series of interactions among different kinds of policies. As a result, the characteristics of the economic system and of economic policies have an implicit content of technology policy, which frequently produces a negative impact on the development of technological capabilities. Therefore, it is imperative to emphasize and deal with the implicit content of technology policy of other development policies, seeking to eliminate possible contradictions, and to make different policies reinforce each other and form a coherent whole, insofar as possible.

Third, the formulation and implementation of a technology policy must have a solid national basis, and an even more limited geographical basis, whenever territorial extension and diversity require it. Government intervention at the national level is essential, and constitutes a prerequisite for international cooperation in this field. Market forces are not enough by themselves to promote technological development, and to ensure its correspondence with socioeconomic objectives. Government action at the national level and by regional and international bodies should be directed toward regulating the importation of technology and reinforcing the bargaining power of technology buyers, promoting interconnections between indigenous technological activities and productive processes, stimulating technological research oriented toward socioeconomic needs, and fostering the development of a technological capacity in the productive sector.

Fourth, policies for technological development cannot ignore the world context within which the economies of Latin America countries operate. Given that Latin America imports almost all of its technology from industrialized countries, it becomes imperative to obtain the best possible advantages from technology suppliers by strengthening the bargaining power of buyers, by establishing government controls, and by developing the capacity to identify, select, and incorporate technology, without stopping the flow of imported technology. In consequence, the development of an indigenous technological capacity must be guided by a strategy of selective interdependence, choosing research fields according to the possibility and convenience of importing technology, the local comparative advantages, the specific needs of the country, and the possibility of exporting the technology that may be produced. At the subregional and regional levels, this can be complemented by a common strategy for the definition of priority areas, and by a greater interconnection and interdependence of the national systems for the production of technology.

Fifth, when formulating and implementing technology policy, it is necessary to act simultaneously on the demand and supply of technology. The traditional viewpoint of science policy, which limits itself to encouraging the generation of knowledge without exploring its possible link with productive activities and development needs, must be overcome. When acting upon the demand for technical knowledge, new interlocutors appear for defining and putting into practice a technology policy. These include, for example, ministries of industry, economics, agriculture and mining, industrial credit organizations, chambers of commerce, professional associations, and other similar institutions. All of this implies the need to establish a new network of institutional interconnections, clearly differentiated from the organizational structure for the traditional science policy, which has been supported mainly by research centers and educational entities.

Sixth, a technological development policy should take into account the characteristics of the different productive sectors and branches. It is not advisable to establish a horizontal policy common to all of them. On the contrary, it is necessary to design a set of flexible policies according to the types of technology involved, the needs for technological activities, the distortions introduced by the ownership structure, the number and size of enterprises, and the characteristics of the technology market. This will lead to a set of vertical policies differentiated according to the branches and sectors of production.

Finally, due to the recent origin of the concept of technology policy, and to the changing pace of external and internal factors that condition it, such policy must be kept flexible and should be implemented gradually. It must have a certain degree of independence, so that it will not be unduly affected by changes in other policies. However, it is also necessary to maintain close coordination and linkage with other development policies in order to avoid

developing an isolated technology policy that would be rendered use-
less. Success in this field will depend to a large extent on the manner in which this dilemma between independence and coordination is
resolved.

LINES OF ACTION FOR TECHNOLOGY POLICY

Taking the principles outlined in the preceding sections as a
base, four main lines of action can be defined for the formulation
and implementation of a technology policy: fostering the demand for
local technology, increasing the technology absorption capacity,
regulating the process of importation of technology, and developing
the production of technology. Action in these four fields must take
place simultaneously, interrelating the phases encompassed by each
and looking for complementaries. Table 5.2 presents a summary
of the main characteristics of each of these lines of action.

Increasing the Demand for Local Technology

Considering that one of the main problems for the development
of an indigenous technological capacity is the lack of demand for local
technology, the first line of action has the objective of increasing
the demand for local technology at the national or regional level,
channeling toward local sources the demand that was previously
oriented toward external sources, and generating more demand for
technological activities related to socioeconomic needs.

Among the policy instruments that can be used for this purpose,
state purchasing power and financing systems deserve special attention. The state, through government agencies, state enterprises,
departments, and so on, is one of the main purchasers of goods and
services in Latin American countries. This purchasing power can
be oriented toward the development of technological capacity through
the direct purchase of research and development services for new
technologies, of engineering and consulting services, and by giving
a preferential treatment to the purchase of goods—particularly capital goods—that incorporate local technology. In this way, an effective demand can be generated which will enable the institutions involved in the production of technology to surpass the minimal critical
mass essential for the efficient performance of these activities.
Furthermore, the use of state purchasing power can be coordinated
at the regional level through intergovernmental agreements.

The leverage of financing agencies in agriculture, industry,
mining, and the like also constitutes an important policy instrument

for increasing the demand for local technology. In fact, the financing of investment projects constitutes perhaps the most effective mechanism to introduce the technological perspective in development planning, and thus the best way of generating a demand for local technology. The use of this instrument requires the explicit incorporation of criteria related to technological development in the evaluation of requests for finance. These criteria should also be extended to the implementation and project execution phase. In addition to including technological criteria for project evaluation, the intervention of financing institutions may be oriented toward the supply of risk capital for the development and improvement of new technologies of local origin; the granting of credit under preferential conditions to users of local technology, including design engineering and consulting services; and the financing of research units in enterprises, of technology research institutes, of specific research programs in existing entities, and other direct means of supporting technological activities. The use of these instruments may be supplemented by legal and administrative measures and incentives, so as to produce a substantial increase in the demand for local technology, an essential condition for technological development.

Increasing the Capacity for Technology Absorption

The objective of the second line of action is to increase the capacity for technology absorption at the enterprise level. In the last analysis, technological progress is expressed through improvements in the production of existing goods and services, or through the creation of new goods and services. The idea is to provide the enterprises with the necessary capacity to better understand the principles of the technology they are using, to master its application, and to introduce modifications that make it more suitable for their specific operating conditions.

Through the effective absorption of technology by enterprises, pressure upon technology suppliers (both local and foreign) can be created, which will force them to improve continuously their technology and the quality of the services they provide. Furthermore, the absorption of imported technology by enterprises requires the initiation of a learning process, and this in turn means that technology will not be imported subsequently in an identical form when the expansion of the enterprise's activities would require it. Therefore, the firm will be in a position to reduce its payments for technology, to widen its sources, to choose better, and to look for local suppliers for certain technological components.

TABLE 5.2

Lines of Action for Technology Policy: Objectives, Instruments, and Support Activities

Line of Action	Objectives	Main Policy Instruments	Support Activities	
			Information System	Training Programs
Promotion of the demand for local technology	Increase the demand for locally generated technology, channeling toward local sources the demand previously oriented to foreign sources, and enhancing the demand for technological activities related to social needs	Measures to motivate enterprises to use local sources of technology (incentives, laws, regulations); use of the leverage of financing organizations to influence enterprises to use local technology; establishment of risk capital funds for local technology users; use of the state purchasing power to promote the purchase of local technical services	Organization of information systems to orient the demand for technology toward local sources (identification of technical opportunities, information on alternative technologies of local origin)	Training of professionals in government, state agencies, and in enterprises to identify and evaluate the possibility of local technologies
Increase in technology absorption capacity	Develop the capacity to absorb technology in the enterprises, dominating its principles, and improving on it continuously (both for imported and local technology)	Disaggregation of the technology to be incorporated into the productive processes; measures to ensure that enterprises perform technological activities (incentives, financing, legal norms); giving support and information on technology to technology users; development of a capacity for engineering design and consultancy	Organization of technical information and extension systems, covering information available at national level and linking it with international sources of information	Training of professionals in enterprises for carrying out technological activities, preparation of technicians to assist the enterprises

86

Regulation of technology imports	Insure the maximum possible benefits from the process of importation of technology, linking it with the generation of local technology, strengthening the bargaining power, and reducing its negative effects	Organization of international searches for technology; disaggregation of imported technology, particularly that linked to large investment projects; state intervention in the process of buying technology through licensing agreements; regulation of international technical cooperation	Organization of information systems on alternative technologies used internationally, on conditions for technology imports, and on local engineering and research capabilities to replace imported technology	Preparation of specialists for disaggregating the technology package, for evaluating alternative technologies, and for the identification of opportunities to replace local for imported technology
Generation of technology	Develop an indigenous capacity for the production of technological knowledge in priority areas related to socioeconomic development objectives (including the adaptation and modification of imported technology)	Organization of research projects oriented toward socioeconomic needs; providing support for the development of an infrastructure of technical research centers; incentives for the generation of technology (credit, fiscal, administrative); establishment of stable sources of finance for technology production; definition of priorities for technological research and organization of a system for planning the generation of technology; generalizing contractual practices for the performance of technological activities	Organization of information systems on research projects under way, of documentation centers, and of equipment, personnel and resources availability for technological research	Training of professionals for the generation of technology, shifting emphasis away from traditional professional, scientific, and technical training that does not seek to solve concrete problems

Source: Compiled by the author.

The main policy instruments in this line of action are the disaggregation of the technological package; the legal and administrative devices that ensure that enterprises perform technological activities; the support, in terms of information, technical assistance, and extension services, that can be given to the enterprise in order to enhance its technical level; and the development of consulting and design engineering capabilities to absorb technology in the cases where it is not possible or convenient that it be done by individual enterprises.

The disaggregation of the technological package—the typical expression of this packaging is the importation of plants on a turnkey basis—is fundamental for the development of a capacity for the absorption of technology, since it leads to a better identification of the components of technical knowledge and their degree of complexity, allowing the enterprise to master the technology it imports. The disaggregation of the technological package occurs generally in two stages: first, a separation of the investment project into each of its modules or components (buildings, installations, licenses, technical assistance, machinery and equipment, and so on); and second, a technical disaggregation as such, where each of the package components is examined from the engineering point of view, differentiating between the medular and peripheral aspects.

The medular component is that which is specific and inherent to the process under study, which distinguishes it from other similar processes or products, and which can assume the form of equipment (special reactor), materials (catalyzer), procedures (operations manuals), designs (circuit specifications), and so on. The peripheral component is generally common to different processes of products (electric installations, unit operations, and the like) and is relatively more freely available than the medular component. It should be noted that the definitions of medular and peripheral technology make sense only for a specific project, and that which is medular in one project can turn out to be peripheral in another. [2]

The legal and administrative devices to promote the performance of technological activities in the enterprise constitute a second instrument to increase the capacity for technology absorption. In fact, the existence of an adequate technical capacity is necessary to insure that the firm will be able to absorb the techniques it uses in its productive activities. When critical-mass reasons preclude the performance of technological activities within the enterprise, the capacity to contract the performance of such activities with specialized institutions (universities, research centers, consulting firms) must be developed. This implies that enterprises should be in a position to define terms of reference, to follow up the progress of the project, and to evaluate its results. For state enterprises it is possible to take direct measures in order to increase the capacity for absorption of technology. In the case of firms not related to the state, regulations such as those set out in the Peruvian General Industrial Law (see Chapter 7), which requires a certain percentage of the net income of enterprises to be devoted to technological research, may be established.

The development of a design engineering and consulting capacity is perhaps the adequate policy instrument to fix, at the national or regional levels, the technological knowledge that cannot be absorbed directly by the enterprise, or whose absorption would be too expensive. For example, certain fields of electrical, chemical, and civil engineering possess characteristics that make it more convenient to support the development of specialized firms to serve the enterprises engaged in production. The same can be applied to feasibility, marketing, and similar studies, which require a degree of specialization that is costly for the average enterprise to acquire. Finally, the organization of information and technical extension services is another mechanism that can help to increase the capacity for absorption of technology, improve the technical level of the firm's personnel, and offer them information on the latest developments in their specific field of interest.

Regulating the Process of Importation
of Technology

The third line of action is oriented toward regulating the process of importation of technology, and its main purpose is to secure the maximum possible advantages from this process, relating it to the production of local technology, increasing the bargaining power of buyers, and reducing the negative effects of technology imports. The main instruments to be used in this field are the organization of international searches for technology, the intervention of government agencies in the purchase of technology, and the regulation of international technical cooperation.

The organization of international searches for technology has the purpose of expanding the information available on some processes or products that are of particular interest for an enterprise or group of enterprises. Through the organization of technology searches it is possible to overcome the traditional passive role of waiting for the technology suppliers to present proposals and to offer technical information to buyers. Buyers can thus be in a position to know the latest developments in their fields, as well as the processes and products still in the experimentation stage. In this way, the range of alternative technologies can be widened, and possible future evolutions can be taken into account when making technical decisions.

A second instrument to regulate the process of importation of technology is the disaggregation of the technological package previously referred to. The main effect of the use of this instrument on the imports of technology is to strengthen the bargaining power of buyers, because of their greater knowledge of the technology to be imported and a detailed analysis of its components. The analysis and evaluation of the imported technology, particularly that related to large investment projects, is a third instrument for this line of action. This evaluation compels the study in greater depth of the set of alternative technologies, in order to define clearly the criteria for making the selection and choosing a particular technology, taking into account not only its effect upon project profitability, but also its impact on the development of an autonomous technological capacity. This evaluation should be made by a government agency, as well as by the firm that is carrying out the investment project.

State intervention in the regulation of technology imports through licensing agreements and the imports of machinery and equipment is another instrument to be used in this line of action. This intervention seeks to avoid the proliferation of restrictive clauses in licensing agreements, to reduce royalty payments, to preclude the insertion of excessive limitations to the licensee in the agreements, and, in general, to strengthen the bargaining power of the users of imported technology. In the case of capital goods imports, there should be a critical analysis of all requests in order to identify the equipment, machinery, or components that can be locally produced. The development of an autonomous technology capacity depends to a large extent on the possibility of producing capital goods, since these incorporate a greater amount of technical know-how and require advanced production techniques, which in turn generate a demand for technological activities, particularly those related to engineering design.

Finally, the regulation of international technical cooperation is another instrument that must be used in this line of action. The technical content of an investment project is frequently defined through the technical assistance provided by international organizations, particularly financial agencies, and by industrialized countries by means of bilateral agreements. The regulation of international technical cooperation covers one of the principal forms of transfer of technical knowledge, especially during the initial stages of formulation of an investment project when many of the parameters that will condition the technology to be applied are determined. On the basis of the assistance provided by experts of a particular country, the technical specifications for a project can be defined so as to drastically reduce the range of possible technology suppliers.

Increasing the Capacity for Generating Technology in Priority Areas

In the fourth place, actions oriented to increase the capacity for generating technology in priority areas also have to be considered. The generation of knowledge must be closely related to the development plans and to the needs of the majority of the population, and should be able to satisfy the demand posed by the production of goods and services.

The main instruments to be used in this line of action are the organization of research and development projects oriented toward the socioeconomic needs, the support of the technical institutional infrastructure, the establishment of sources of finance and incentives for technological research, the generalization of contractual practices, and the implementation of a planning system for technological activities.

The organization of specific projects related to the problems of the productive system and of the country's needs will steer technological research toward social interest objectives, avoiding the traditional isolation of the scientific community. The research project and the research program, with precise objectives and with estimates of their possible impact upon the problem area under consideration, should become the basic unit for organizing technology production activities.[3] The standardization of contractual practices to channel state support for research and the establishment of new financing sources will operate in the same manner. In all of these cases, the instrument will lead to the rationalization of activities related to the production of local technology, providing a framework to assure their congruence with economic development objectives, social needs, and the requirements of the productive system.

Other instruments to be used in this line of action refer to the measures taken to promote the development and consolidation of the infrastructure of technological research institutes. These include programs to support existing organizations (such as the provision of equipment, working capital, and training programs) or actions geared to the creation of new institutions. Here are found also the schemes (credit, tax, administrative, and so on) used as incentives for enterprises, engineering firms, and research centers that perform technological activities of interest to the country.

Finally, in order to rationalize technology production it is essential to develop a planning system for technological research, with the purpose of defining priorities, allocating resources, and dividing the workload among the various institutions that perform technological activities.

It should be noted that the concept of local generation of production of technology used in this study includes the adaptation and modification of imported technology, whether for use at the national level or for reexport.

Even though each policy instrument has been associated with a line of action, it must be pointed out that there is no one-to-one correspondence between lines of action and instruments, and that an instrument may help in attaining the goals of several lines of action. For example, the dissagregation of the technological package strengthens the bargaining power of buyers and helps to regulate the imports of technology; it allows the identification of these components of imported technology that can be produced locally, thus generating a demand for technological activities, and it also permits the users to have a greater understanding of the characteristics of imported technology, thus facilitating its absorption. In a similar manner, the establishment of stable sources of finance for research projects oriented toward socioeconomic objectives is an instrument that promotes the demand for local technology and the production of technology. The examples of multiple use of policy instruments may be extended, although it is possible to identify a main line of action to which a specific instrument is related. The problem of technology policy instruments in underdeveloped countries, and in Latin America in particular, is very complex and requires further analysis and study.[4]

Table 5.2 also contains a summary of the main support activities that are necessary in the fields of information and training, relating each of them to the proposed lines of action. The set of information activities constitutes, in turn, a new line of action for the formulation and implementation of policies for technological development. The same can be applied to training programs.

From an analysis of the lines of action, their objectives and instruments, and the support activities, it can be appreciated that there is a need for technology to become an integral part of the development planning effort. On the one hand, this implies planning for technological activities, and on the other hand, inserting the perspective of technology into the formulation of development plans. It is also necessary to stress that technological domination aggravates underdevelopment, and that the plans and policies in other areas frequently contain negative implicit measures with regard to technology, which in the long run undermine efforts to overcome underdevelopment.

ACTIVATING TECHNOLOGY POLICIES*

As mentioned earlier, the art or science of designing technology policies is relatively well advanced in Latin America. There are more than 500 studies containing recommendations on what to do about importing technological capabilities, and these are often based on empirical data that show why technological capabilities have not been widely developed. However, when coming to the implementation of these policies, there is a shortage of material giving actual experiences. It appears as if policy-making efforts are made in isolation from decision makers who shape the development of technical capabilities. Thus entrepreneurs, government officials, researchers, and professionals often do not pay attention to technology policies and their behavior is not significantly affected by them. This has been the case primarily because the instruments and mechanisms required to implement technology policies have been ignored by those who formulate policies. In the few cases where policy instruments have been designed and implemented, they have often been blocked by other and more powerful policy instruments, which operated in a way contrary to technology policy objectives.

At the national or industry level, technological behavior is the result of aggregating decisions on technology made by enterprises, research centers, and government agencies. As usually happens with matters of this complexity, the overall technological behavior is more than just the sum of its parts. The technical capabilities of industry are the result of interactions among many types of technological decisions made by different agents at several levels, as well as decisions that do not have the direct purpose of affecting technical capabilities, but that condition technological development in an indirect way.

The problem of activating technology policies thus consists of designing and operating the policy instruments that orient technological behavior—the systematic aggregation of technological decisions—in the direction specified by the objectives of technology policy.

---

*This section borrows heavily from the work of Bertram Gross in reports such as "Activating National Plans," in Bertram Gross, ed., Action Under Planning (New York: McGraw Hill, 1967); and "The Limits of Development Administration," paper presented at the United Nations Interregional Seminar on Organization and Administration of Development Planning Agencies, Kiev, October 1972.

This is a process that must bridge the gap between policy making at the government (macro) level, and decision making at the enterprise or research center (micro) level.

Several factors intervene in the process of designing and operating policy instruments. The diagram in Figure 5.1 shows the main elements that should be taken into account.

Policies for technology in the real world are the result of complex interactions between what are called explicit and implicit technology policies, and not a simple translation of technology objectives into criteria for government decision making. If, on the other hand, there are present the objectives and criteria that lead to the formulation of explicit technology policies, it is necessary to recognize that, on the other hand, there are many other objectives and criteria for the formulation of other policies (industrial, financial, labor, foreign trade, and so on) that have an important impact on technological decisions. There is a need for uncovering the implications of other policies in order to assess the direction that the real policy resulting from the interaction between implicit and explicit policies will take.

There have already been some examples of this process of explicating implicit technology policies that show the power of these concepts.[5] It has often been found that contradictions emerge between the aims of explicit and implicit technology policies, and that the resultant policy contains many components of contradictory nature whose predominance will be determined by the relative strength of the policy instrument used to implement it. For example, it is generally recognized that fiscal incentives for the performance of research and development in industry are a relatively weak instrument in comparison with credit mechanisms that motivate the entrepreneur to acquire technology abroad. It is clear that the component of the resultant policy that promotes the import of technology will prevail over the component that promotes the development of local technology.

Figure 5.1 also points out that technological decisions made by enterprises determine the technology absorption capacity of the country, as well as the pattern of demand for technology. The decisions made by research centers and engineering firms determine the internal supply of technology, while the decisions of foreign suppliers of technology (consultants, multinational enterprises, licensers, suppliers of equipment, and so on) determine the external supply of technology. Among the factors conditioning the decisions made by each of these actors are the policy instruments employed by government. The crucial problem in the design and operation of a particular instrument is that of determining its relative influence on the decisions taken by these actors. Unless this is known with a

FIGURE 5.1

Issues in Technology Policy Formulation and Implementation

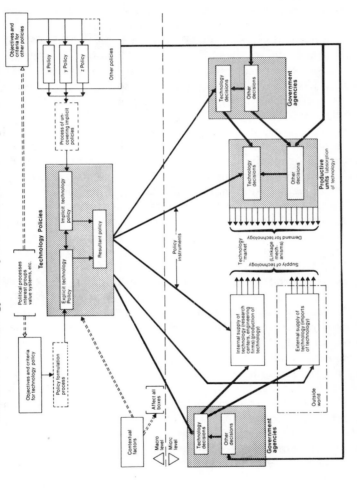

Source: Constructed by the author.

95

degree of certainty, it will be virtually impossible to anticipate the actual effect and impact of a particular policy and its corresponding policy instruments.[6] (See Chapter 4.)

However, in matters of technology policy, as with everything else, it is not sufficient to have good policies and policy instruments, for these do not exist independently of the individuals who design and wield them. In order to introduce substantial changes and modifications that will lead to the attainment of desired objectives, it is necessary to have access to political power. This may appear a rather simplistic observation, except that all too often there is a tendency to forget that reason alone is not sufficient to bring about desired changes. Unfortunately the instances in which politicians have paid significant attention to technology matters and in which those knowledgeable in the field have held positions of responsibility are rather few.

Furthermore, in the cases where access to political power has been secured, it has been accompanied by difficult battles against those proposing other policies that run contrary to the objectives of enhancing technical capabilities and attaining a capacity for autonomous decision making in matters of technology. The record is uneven in different countries, in the same country at different times, and in different sectors and agencies of the same country. Neverthless, by and large, actual changes have been rather meager in comparison to the grandiose designs that are often offered for technology policy. It is only in the late 1970s that the situation has changed significantly enough in a number of Latin American countries to warrant a measure of optimism.

Relating conceptual frameworks to action requires several conditions that must be satisfied simultaneously. First, there must be a core of trained people who combine executive talent with political sensitivity and with intellectual leadership. Second, it is necessary for the group to have political access and discretionary power, which means that those in charge of implementing technology policies will be able to carry out the measures they consider necessary, even when opposed by other interest groups, because of the confidence and the support they receive from top government officials. Third, sufficient funds must be made available, if possible independent of the vagaries of budgetary negotiations, so that their operation is guaranteed for at least five years. Fourth, the group must have a clear concept of the problem and a thorough knowledge of the industrial, scientific, technical, educational, etc., situation of the country, preferably acquired through systematic studies of both empirical and theoretical nature. Finally, the core group, and particularly its leaders, must have a capacity for designing and operating policy instruments in such a way as to balance short-term achievements—the delivery-goods aspect—with the attainment of long-term objectives. If the emphasis goes too much in one direction or another, the group will either become immersed exclusively in day-to-day operational problems, or concentrate only on long-term payoffs with the consequent loss of political support. Perhaps the small number of cases where technology policies have been successfully designed and implemented results from the difficulty of combining all of these conditions at the same time.

NOTES

1. See The Science and Technology Policy Instruments Project (Ottawa: IDRC, 1975).

2. On this issue, see Charles Cooper and Francisco Sercovich, The Channels and Mechanisms for the Transfer of Technology from Developed to Developing Countries (Geneva: UNCTAD, 1971); and Desagregación del Paquete Tecnológico (Lima: Grupo de Tecnología, Junta del Acuerdo de Cartagena, 1974). On the limits of technological unpackaging see Charles Cooper and Philip Maxwell, Machinery Suppliers and the Transfer of Technology to Latin America, Science Policy Research Unit, Sussex University, 1975.

3. On this issue, see Joyce Sabato, Empresas y Fábricas de Tecnología (Washington, D.C.: Department of Scientific Affairs, OAS, 1972); and Manual para la Presentación y Ejecución de Proyectos de Investigación Tecnológica Industrial, 2nd ed. (Lima: ITINTEC, 1975).

4. On this matter, see the reports of The Science and Technology Policy Instruments (STPI) Project (Ottawa: IDRC, 1978).

5. See, for example, the reports on the feasibility studies for the STPI project, and in particular the paper by Gustavo Flores, Isaías Flit, and Francisco Sagasti, "Instrumentos de Política Tecnológica Implícita en Planes de Desarrollo y Leyes Generales en el Perú" (Lima: 1972). Mimeographed. See also the Main Comparative Report of the STPI Project (Ottawa: IDRC, 1978).

6. See Alberto Araoz and Francisco Sagasti, Methodological Guidelines for Science and Technology Policy Instruments (STPI) Project (Ottawa: IDRC, 1976), for a further examination of these concepts.

6

Technology Policies in the Andean Common Market

INTRODUCTION

The five countries of the Andean Common Market--Bolivia, Colombia, Ecuador, Peru, and Venezuela (Chile was a member of the Andean Pact from its formation until it withdrew in 1976)--have many common characteristics that go back several hundred years. Even before the arrival of the Spanish conquerors, the Andean region was the site of an advanced civilization that encompassed part of Colombia, Ecuador, Peru, Bolivia, and Chile. The colonial administration reinforced these links during the sixteenth, seventeenth, and eighteenth centuries by making the vice-royalty of Peru responsible for the affairs of the Spanish crown in most of Latin America, particularly the Andean countries.

The tradition of Hispanic dominance of colonial times, which was continued with relatively few changes during the first hundred years of independence, fostered the development of the liberal arts professions and the predominance of scholastic and intellectual university careers, to the detriment of engineering and applied sciences. This tradition continues even in the 1970s, in spite of the changes imposed by rapid industrialization. Scientific activities during colonial times and most of the postindependence period were weak; they were oriented primarily toward descriptive studies, and constituted an appendix to the intellectual life of colonial powers. Barring a few notable exceptions, particularly in medicine, the general picture until the 1900s shows local scientific and techno-

---

Used with permission from Chapter 2 in Mauricio Guerrero and Francisco Sagasti, <u>El Desarollo Científico y Tecnológico de América Latina</u> (Buenos Aires: BID/INTAL, 1974).

logical activities developing slowly, in a disjoined way and without effective support.

Although the university system developed extensively during colonial times (particularly in Peru and Colombia), it was not until the late 1800s that engineering was taught in the universities. Toward the end of the nineteenth century the pressure of positivism helped to modify considerably the scholastic orientation of higher education toward experimental science, which in turn helped to foster a more favorable environment for practical careers. Nevertheless, by the mid-1970s, the importance of engineering and technical professions had not yet been fully acknowledged in the Andean countries. As an illustration, between 1950 and 1970, during a rapid increase of the university population in Peru, the relative share of engineering, science, and technical professions fell from 17 percent to 10 percent of the student population.

INDUSTRIALIZATION IN THE ANDEAN PACT
COUNTRIES AND ITS IMPACT ON
TECHNOLOGY POLICY

During the 1930s the Andean Pact countries embarked on a process of industrialization, prompted by balance-of-payments difficulties and the Great Depression of 1929. Industrialization efforts, which accelerated after World War II, reaching a peak in the early 1960s, were characterized by an import-substitution orientation aimed at satisfying an internal demand for consumer and light durable goods out of local production rather than through imports.

The industrialization process began to impose some strains on the incipient technological capabilities of the Andean Pact countries, which were incapable of responding adequately to the new demands posed by the rapid development of industry. The university was not prepared to train the technicians and engineers required for the industrialization process and could not perform research and development activities of direct relevance to industry. Local engineering consultancy services were practically nonexistent, and most of the technical requirements of industry were satisfied through technology imports. The fact that industries were frequently established in association with foreign enterprises reinforced this trend, for it was more convenient to import equipment, experts, technology, and methods of production than to develop them locally.

Nevertheless, the industrialization process generated demand for some specific scientific and technological activities. First among these was the provision of technical norms and standards. Since equipment and processes were imported from a variety of countries that used different measuring systems and followed different standards, the production of intermediate goods was often uncoordinated, and many difficulties emerged when inputs of a particular industry depended on outputs from another. This spurred the creation of technical norms and standards institutes to introduce some order into industrial production.

Industrial enterprises were also worried about the lack of well-trained engineers and managers, and pressed universities-- particularly the institutes of technical education--to expand the student body and to upgrade the quality of education in engineering. Many technical careers were started in universities, and several polytechnic institutes were created, for example, the Universidad Técnica del Estado in Chile and the Escuela de Ingeniería Técnica in Peru.

Furthermore, Andean Pact countries became concerned about industrial productivity, as well as about technical standards and human resources. After the initial years when production could be expanded easily to satisfy the internal market at a profit, industrialists often found that they had invested in plants that exceeded the capacity of the local market, and that competition from new enterprises established behind the tariff barriers threatened their placid existence. At this stage productivity centers emerged in most of the Andean countries and industrial engineering became one of the most popular technical careers.

In the middle and late 1960s attention shifted in the direction of science, pushing the concern for technical standards, productivity, and human resources to a lower plane. National councils for science and technology were established in four of the Andean countries, partly as a result of the intervention of international agencies such as UNESCO and the Organization of American States (OAS). The exceptions were Ecuador and Bolivia, where the scientific community had not grown enough to exert pressure. The national councils, and the scientists, administrators, and advisors behind them, pushed for increases in the supply of resources to scientific research, arguing that one of the main bottlenecks of the development process was the lack of an indigenous scientific and technological capacity. Their efforts were crowned with moderate success, particularly in Colombia, Venezuela, and Chile, where the national councils exerted considerable influence on the orientation of science. The situation was not so favorable in Peru because the National Research Council was not given the necessary power and resources to carry out the functions assigned to it by law.

In parallel with the emergence of the national councils for science and technology, a series of studies on the conditions and characteristics of the process of transfer of technology to the Andean countries was begun under the sponsorship of the Department of Scientific Affairs of the OAS. These studies,[1] focused primarily on transfer of technology through licensing agreements, showed that in most instances agreements were accompanied by clauses and conditions that were unfavorable to the recipient countries. This realization in turn gave rise to efforts aimed at regulating the inflow of foreign technology, particularly through licensing agreements, and also provided an additional reason to impose some controls on the inflow of foreign capital.

The Andean Common Market was established in 1969 through the Acuerdo de Caragena (Cartagena Greeement), following two and a half years of negotiations among the six countries.[2] Venezuela did not sign the agreement until 1973, when it joined the common market after several years of participation as an active observer, and Chile withdrew in 1976. Thus the five Andean countries (Bolivia, Colombia, Ecuador, Peru, and Venezuela) have an economic integration scheme that combines reductions in tariffs for trade in the Andean region, a set of common external tariffs for trade with countries outside the common market, a joint scheme for planning industrial production in selected industries, procedures for harmonizing economic and social policies, and a mechanism for coordinating their technology policies.[3]

The structure provided by the Comisión del Acuerdo de Cartagena (Commission of the Cartagena Agreement)--the Junta del Acuerdo de Cartagena, which is the executive secretariat, and the various councils advising these two organs--is complemented by several other agreements binding the six Andean countries. The most important of these with respect to science policy is the Convenio Andrés Bello (Andres Bello Agreement), which was signed by the ministers of education of the Andean countries. This agreement aims at coordinating the educational systems through the establishment of degree equivalences, the promotion of joint educational programs, and the organization of collaborative research activities in the universities. The secretariat of the Andres Bello agreement has been less active than the Junta del Acuerdo de Cartagena, and its impact on science and technology policy in the Andean region has been rather limited.

SCIENCE AND TECHNOLOGY IN THE ANDEAN PACT COUNTRIES

The science and technology system of the Andean countries presents four main characteristics: an imbalance in the flows of imported and local technology, structural deficiencies in the organization

of scientific and technological activities, negative impact of indiscriminate technology imports, and isolation of the university from
the scientific and technical needs of society. Each will be analyzed
in turn. [4]

Imbalance in the Flow of Imported
and Local Technology

Most productive activities in the Andean countries are based
on the use of foreign technology. This is particularly true of manufacturing and extractive industries and the modern segments of agriculture. The main exception is the subsistence of traditional agricultural activities which are based on local technologies that have
evolved slowly over several hundred years. Although the latter still
employ a large percentage of the population in a few of the Andean
countries (notably Bolivia, Peru, and Ecuador), they contribute
relatively little to economic growth.

There are several indicators of this relative imbalance in technology flows. For all the Andean countries, expenditures for foreign
technology--in the form of royalties, payments for technical assistance, and payments for other elements of technical knowledge--
vastly exceed expenditures on research and development. In Peru,
for example, the ratio of payments for imported technology to expenditures for research and development in 1969 was approximately
2 to 1, while in most Western European countries and Japan it was
between 1 to 10 and 1 to 20, and in the United States 1 to 240. [5]

Another indicator of the relative preponderance of imported
technology is the number of patents registered by foreigners. Between 1960 and 1969 the proportion of patents held by foreigners in
Chile, Peru, and Venezuela increased, reaching at least 95 percent.
Although patents are not a very reliable indicator of technology flows,
they do give an idea of the extent to which national inventive activities
are overwhelmed by technology imports. The breakdown of imports
into consumer, intermediate, and capital goods provides another indicator. The majority of the Andean Common Market countries import most of their capital goods, which embody technology to a greater extent than intermediate or consumer goods; in 1970, for example,
Peru imported more than 70 percent of its capital goods.

Structural Deficiencies in the Organization of
Scientific and Technological Activities

Until 1968 there was little empirical information on science
and technology in Latin America; after 1968 data-gathering activities

began to provide a general picture of the structure of the scientific and technological system.[6]

With respect to the magnitude of the national effort in science and technology in the Andean countries, it is known that in 1970 Bolivia had approximately 110 research institutions and about 1,100 scientists, technicians, and auxiliary personnel involved in research. Colombia had 230 organizations and about 1,500 researchers. Figures for Chile were on the order of 186 organizations with 2,200 researchers. Peru had approximately 184 organizations with 2,200 researchers, technicians, and administrative personnel. For Venezuela the figures were 194 research institutions with 1,900 full-time equivalent researchers. Figures for Ecuador report 50 institutions with a total of 1,600 scientific and technological personnel; these latter figures are inaccurate, however, in the sense that they include professors at universities who are not directly engaged in research. While the data point out that in total the Andean Pact countries have approximately 900 research institutions and approximately 11,000 researchers, the figures must be taken with caution because of the deficiencies involved in this first comparative exercise in gathering science and technology statistics. It is quite likely that approximately half of the 900 research institutions recorded are not concerned with research and development on a full and continuous basis; and that of the 11,000 researchers, technicians, and auxiliary personnel, only one-half to one-third are actually involved full time in research and development activities. Finally, the total expenditures on research and development for 1970 were around 100 million U.S. dollars. However, if educational activities were omitted, the amount certainly would be reduced by at least one-quarter or one-third.

It has been estimated that a minimum of 10,000 full-time researchers and approximately $100 million in current expenditures were required to sustain a viable scientific and technological system in any country in the early 1970s.[7] This would imply that the Andean countries as a whole were just below the critical mass required, and that no country would be capable of sustaining a viable scientific and technological system on its own. Figures on average current expenditures per institution vary greatly, although they remain in the range between $50,000 and $150,000 per year. There is also some information on the number of research projects under way in Peru and Venezuela in 1970, showing that average expenditures per project are around $5,000 for Peru and $7,000 for Venezuela, and that the average number of researchers per project was 1.7 for Peru and 0.7 for Venezuela.

All the available information indicates that the Andean countries have a rather small and fragmented scientific and technological

system, that collectively they barely meet the minimum requirements for a viable scientific and technological system, and that individually they fall well below them.

There are also problems associated with the quality of the
manpower in science and technology. For example, a survey of the
seven major research institutions in Peru revealed that less than 10
percent of the personnel had had more than two years of postgraduate
training at universities in Peru or abroad, indicating that the pool of
highly qualified scientists and technicians to head projects is rather
small, and that qualitative deficiencies in existing personnel may be
even more acute and difficult to overcome than quantitative deficiencies in the number of researchers.

Turning to the orientation and the setting of research institutions, it is known that more than 40 percent are directly or indirectly
dependent on government support. [8] Moreover, there is an imbalance
in the location of the research personnel and the allocation of funds;
although universities account for most of the research centers and
scientific personnel, they account for a relatively smaller proportion
of total research and development expenditures. More detailed
analyses of available figures indicate that the majority of expenditures in research and development are oriented toward support activities, with a smaller proportion being spent on research activities
proper. With the exception of agriculture, most fields do not receive a substantial share of the funds allocated to science and technology, which are spread among the social sciences, the humanities,
basic sciences (mathematics, physics, chemistry), and to a lesser
extent, medicine. Engineering activities receive a fairly small percentage of funds.

On the basis of the limited information available it is possible
to conclude that several structural deficiencies exist in the organization of scientific and technological activities in the Andean countries;
namely, that the scientific and technological effort of these countries
is below the minimum critical mass both in quantitative and qualitative terms, that it is excessively fragmented, that it is oriented toward activities not directly relevant to the development problems,
that it is heavily dependent on government support, and that it is not
integrated into a coherent system at either the national or the regional level.

Negative Impact of Indiscriminate Technology Imports

Information gathered between 1968 and 1972 on technology importation in the Andean Pact countries indicates that it is not contributing effectively to the development of local technological capabil-

ities.[9] It is widely acknowledged that the imported technology does not necessarily correspond to the prevalent needs, in the sense that large-scale, capital-intensive technologies are used in situations where smaller-scale production and lower capital investment would be adequate. Imported technologies are usually based on intermediate inputs and raw materials that are unavailable locally and often require highly skilled manpower, which is scarce in the region.

Most of the available information documents extensively the unfavorable conditions under which technology imports take place in the Andean countries. To the explicit costs of technology transfer-- which include royalties, technical assistance, and other payments stipulated in the contracts--it is necessary to add the implicit costs derived from overpricing of intermediate inputs, underpricing of exports, and various additional payments that are usually not explicit. This means that the total cost of technology imports for the Andean countries exceeds the actual recorded costs involved in licensing and contractual arrangements. Furthermore, it is also necessary to consider the implicit costs involved in the import of capital and machinery, for which no reliable data are available. Although the available information is rather scattered and fragmented, it is estimated that in the early 1970s the Andean countries spent twice as much for foreign technology as for investment in research and development, although it is quite likely that this ratio may be even higher.

In addition to the high costs involved in technology transfer, studies of licensing agreements in the Andean Pact countries reveal a proliferation of restrictive clauses that have effectively limited the capacity of the recipient firm to use for its own purposes and benefits the technology being imported. Restrictive clauses regarding the destination of exports, the selection of intermediate inputs, or the pricing of final products, for example, have turned out to be common in most licensing agreements, indicating that the decision-making autonomy of the recipient firm has been curtailed through the import of foreign technology.

The structure of the process of technology importation at the beginning of the 1970s was such that inadequate technologies were being imported, high costs were being paid, and autonomy in decision making was lost by the recipient of foreign technology. This was a situation that the regulations promulgated by the commission of the Andean Common Market and the national governments set out to change.

Isolation of the University from Scientific
and Technological Needs of Society

Until the early 1970s the universities in the Andean countries were divorced from the actual needs of the productive system. This traditional isolation was a matter for concern, particularly because the greatest concentration of intellectual, scientific, and technological manpower was in the universities. Furthermore, the continuous crisis that most of the universities in the Andean countries had experienced since the middle 1960s had prevented them from reorienting their own activities and contributing effectively to the development effort. This situation was aggravated by the extreme dependence of some universities on centers of higher education in advanced countries (particularly the United States), in the sense that they structured their curricula and courses around foreign models of little relevance to Andean conditions and received substantial foreign aid. (See the discussion in Chapter 8 on the possible contribution of universities to scientific and technological development in Latin America.)

During 1969 and 1970 university unrest in Venezuela, Colombia, and Peru disrupted normal educational processes. This was also the case in Chile from 1971 to 1973 although the crisis reached catastrophic proportions with the right-wing military coup in 1973. The Bolivian and the Ecuadorian universities have not been able to remain aloof from the social changes their countries have been undergoing. As a result disruptions in university life, added to the traditional lack of concern for the scientific and technical needs of the development process, have prevented the universities from contributing effectively to the development of the Andean countries.

The overall diagnosis of the scientific and technological system in the Andean countries is rather pessimistic and shows that major changes are required before the system can become an effective contributor to the development process. Some reforms being put into effect include restructuring the scientific and technological system in some Andean countries, integrating the science and technology system with productive and social needs, reducing the isolation of universities, and promoting more intensive cooperation among the Andean countries.

TECHNOLOGY POLICY EFFORTS IN
THE ANDEAN PACT COUNTRIES

In examining the structure of science and technology policies in the Andean countries it is necessary to consider two levels--that of national policies and that of regional agreements--which are effected primarily through the commission of the Andean Common Market and put into practice by the countries themselves and the secretariat of the Andean Common Market (Junta del Acuerdo de Cartagena). Both levels will be considered in examining each of the four substantive areas for the formulation and implementation of science and technology policies in the Andean Pact countries.

Regulating the Inflow of Foreign Technology

The regulation of the inflow of foreign technology, particularly via licensing agreements, started in the Andean Pact countries in Colombia in 1968 through the enactment of Decree Law 444 of March 22, 1967, which at the same time reestablished the control of foreign exchange in Colombia. The main provision of this law from the point of view of technology transfer is the requirement that government approve all licensing agreements taking place between Colombian and foreign firms before payments in foreign exchange can be authorized. The Royalties Committee, as it is called in the law, works in coordination with the several agencies in charge of administering exports and imports, foreign exchange, and foreign investment. Its main functions were originally to take care that licensing agreements not contain restrictive clauses of any type, to make explicit the commitments of the licensor, and to ensure that the licensee receives the relevant information from the licensor in order to utilize and fully absorb the technology matter of the contract. The committee analyzes the cost of the technology being imported and approves the form of payment.

Chile started this mechanism for the regulation of technology imports in July 1967, when the Council of the Central Bank of Chile (the organization in charge of authorizing foreign exchange remittances) decided to create a committee to revise licensing agreements. It was established that the contracts should be registered at the Central Bank and be approved by the executive council prior to sending foreign exchange payments abroad.

The Royalties Committee in Colombia and the Advisory Committee to Revise Licensing Agreements in Chile were the forerunners of legislation approved by the Andean Pact commission as part of Decision 24 in December 1970. Decision 24 concerns foreign investment, licensing agreements, and transfer of technology in general, and seeks to regulate the way in which foreign investment is to be made in the Andean Pact, to stipulate the types of acceptable clauses in the licensing agreements, and to'structure a general set of policies for regulating the inflow of foreign technology. Decision 24 followed the rationale that there is a close interconnection between foreign investment and transfer of technology.

Decision 24 created several government agencies in each of the countries to register transfer of technology agreements and put into practice the policies regarding the importation of technology.

This meant that the existing institutions in Chile and Colombia, which were directed primarily at reducing the costs of technology transfer, were expanded to consider broader aspects. In the case of Bolivia, Ecuador, and Peru, this implied the creation of new organizations, and the same was true in Venezuela, which joined the Andean Common Market at a later stage. These agencies are supposed to evaluate, authorize, and approve all contracts referring to commercialization of technology and those related to the use of the elements of industrial property (patents, trademarks, industrial models, industrial designs). This reinforces the bargaining power of national firms that acquire foreign technology, and also allows the introduction of considerations regarding national objectives into the process of technology transfer.

Decision 24 also refers to specific conditions that are acceptable for technology transfer at the Andean level. Article 6 stipulates the clauses that cannot be accepted in licensing agreements; Article 21 stipulates that firms cannot capitalize the technology contribution and consider it part of foreign investment, and it also forbids the payment of royalties between the subsidiaries or affiliates and their headquarters.

To improve the information available on commercialization of technology, and consequently to increase the bargaining power of the recipient countries, Article 48 establishes a system for the permanent exchange of information on the terms and effects of technology purchases. The basic idea is that one country will not be subjected to conditions differing widely from those for another, allowing the implementation of a type of most-favored-nation principle in the acquisition of technology.

Articles 20 and 25 establish for the first time a legal frame for limiting restrictive practices resulting from the purchase of technology. Clauses that impose constraints on exports, tie the agreements to the purchase of inputs and raw materials, give the licensor some control over the structure of production or personnel contracting, and that constrain the utilization of the technology after the expiration of the licensing agreement are eliminated through these two articles. Articles 26 and 54 determine that common regulations on industrial property will be adopted in the Andean Common Market.

Finally, Articles 22, 23, and 55 established a mandate for the commission to approve a common program on technology policies in the Andean region. This program was approved through Decision 84 in June 1974. It contains a declaration outlining the overall strategy for technology policy in the Andean region and creates several instruments for the implementation of such policies. Therefore, at the Andean level, Decisions 24, 85, and 84 establish a general structure for regulating the inflow of foreign technology, increasing bargaining power, reducing the cost of technology transfer, and obtaining the greatest benefits from the technology acquired abroad.

All the countries of the Andean region have already passed legislation to implement Decision 24. A series of government agencies (Oficinas Nacionales Competentes) has been created to evaluate and approve agreements for technology transfer. However, the necessary exchange of information and the training of personnel involved in these offices have been somewhat limited, which has impaired the effective application of these regulations. At present there is a proposal under consideration, submitted by the secretariat of the Andean Common Market to the commission and to experts from the six countries, that deals with the progressive establishment of an information system at the level of the Andean Pact, covering not only the aspects referring to transfer of technology but also those dealing with the generation of technology.

Promoting the Demand for Local Technology
and Increasing the Absorption Capacity of
the Productive System

A series of programs designed to promote the absorption of technology and to increase the demand for local technology was started in the early 1970s. The most important of these is the one originated in Peru by the Instituto de Investigación Tecnológica Industrial y de Normas Técnicas (ITINTEC).[10] See Chapter 7. Through the ITINTEC system all enterprises in the industrial sector must set aside for industrial research 2 percent of net income before taxes. In case they decide not to use the funds for research, or in case the program they submit is not approved by ITINTEC, this 2 percent will go to a central fund administered by ITINTEC for the purpose of furthering industrial technological activities. The system has motivated enterprises to organize research and troubleshooting activities to help solve technical problems. Given that the enterprise can either do the research on its own premises or contract it out, this has also meant increased interaction between the institutions involved in technical fields and the productive sector. Through the increased awareness of the importance of technology and the realization of scientific and technological activities, the ITINTEC system has also helped increase the technology absorption capacity of enterprises.

Another program to promote demand for local technology was under consideration in 1975 in Colombia. It would operate through a system that would systematically orient government procurement toward the purchase of goods that are manufactured with local technology and the direct purchase of local engineering and technical services. It is expected to increase the demand for local technology. In Colombia the laws have been passed to implement these goals. Similar programs are being organized, although on a smaller scale, in Venezuela and Peru, in the latter case through the use of national technical norms and standards that would be enforced in government purchases.

The joint sectoral industrial programming system of the Andean Common Market also provides an opportunity for organizing a systematic search for local technology, for starting programs to increase the supply of technology, as well as programs for assuring that the technology that must be imported is absorbed at the enterprise level.

Increasing Relevant Research and
Development Activities

Decision 84, which establishes the basis for a common technology policy in the Andean Pact countries, creates the Programas Andinos de Desarrollo Tecnológico (PADT: Andean Programs for Technological Development). The PADTs take the form of joint research efforts by institutions of two or more countries in the Andean region, which pool their resources, facilities, and information for the solution of a common technological problem. In 1975 there were two PADTs under way, one in the area of metallurgical processing of copper, lead, and zinc ores and the other in the area of the utilization of tropical forests for industrial purposes; and another was being organized in the food industries area.

The PADTs also provide for a variety of cooperation agreements that are not exclusively directed to research and development but do encompass training programs, exchange of information, coordination of ongoing activities, and a variety of other efforts for the promotion of local technological capabilities.

In addition to the work of the secretariat of the Andean Common Market, and after several years of rather ineffective attempts, the secretariat of the Convenio Andres Bello in 1977 launched several joint research projects. These cover areas such as metallurgy, food processing, control of marine pollution, and the improvement of traditional technologies, although their results are not likely to be seen until at least 1980.

Several national programs have also been instituted to promote and increase the performance of research and development activities. The ITINTEC system in Peru is one of these, having increased the total amount of funds available for industrial research from approximately half a million U.S. dollars in the late 1960s to over ten million U.S. dollars in the middle 1970s. Venezuela is also rapidly and systematically expanding the funds and the number of projects involved in industrial research. It has been able to apply a significant percentage of its oil revenues to the development of a local scientific and technological infrastructure, emphasizing research activities. Colombia, too, has increased the number of research programs under way, trying to link them to the national priorities established in the development plan, particularly in the field of nutrition and food.

Promoting Scientific and Technological Human Resources

With the exception of Venezuela, which has launched a massive ten-year, multimillion-dollar program for the preparation of human resources, the Andean Pact countries have not given preferential attention to the preparation of technological manpower for research and development or other technological activities. This has meant that the existing programs to regulate the inflow of foreign technology, to promote the demand and absorption of technology, and to increase research and development activities have relied to a very large extent on the existing pool of human resources.

During the first stages of the programs to improve technological capabilities in the Andean region, the lack of human resources has not proved to be the acute bottleneck that was once thought. However, as programs advance it is likely that by the end of the 1970s this may become the most important limitation. This will be aggravated because there are no substantial efforts being made at present in the Andean countries for the improvement of scientific and technological education.[11]

PROSPECTS FOR A COMMON TECHNOLOGY POLICY IN THE ANDEAN PACT

The efforts made by the Andean Pact to establish a common technology policy were the first of their kind ever attempted by a group of underdeveloped countries. For this reason they have an importance that exceeds the boundaries of the Andean region and merit careful attention by other Third World countries. However, it is necessary to keep in mind that most of the technology policy measures were adopted and put into practice in the early 1970s, and that a full evaluation of their impact must wait at least one decade.

Nevertheless, it is possible to offer some preliminary appreciations of the way in which the design and implementation of the common technology policy has been progressing, and to venture some ideas regarding their future.

The prospects for a common technology policy in the Andean countries are conditioned by the future of the common market itself, and any crisis in the integration scheme will affect the design and implementation of technology policies. This was clearly the case during 1974-76, when the Andean Pact went through its worst crisis in its short history. [12] The impact of the crisis on technology policy was felt primarily through the unfavorable climate for the presentation, discussion, and approval of proposals, and also through the delays in the approval of the joint programas sectoriales de desarrollo industrial (sectoral industrial development programs), to which some of the proposals on technology policies were linked. On the other hand, and even though only three programas Andinos de desarrollo tecnológico (Andean technological development programs) were organized during 1974-76, their technical success and economic impact have shown it is possible to continue work on specific technology policy activities at the same time that other mechanisms of the integration scheme are under criticism and revision. Nevertheless, the failure to establish the much needed Andean technological information system, after more than four years of protracted discussions and negotiations, has not helped to dispel the skepticism about a common technology policy on the part of many professionals, scientists, policy makers and entrepreneurs in the Andean region.

At the root of these difficulties in the design and implementation of a common technology policy lie the inherent tensions and conflicts between national and regional interests in any integration scheme. In the case of the Andean Pact, these tensions, which grew as the crisis became more pronounced, were also heightened by conflicting perceptions on the part of national government officials and of the secretariat of the common market staff regarding the role of the common technology policy and the relative weight of national and regional objectives, programs, and agencies.

A common technology policy for countries taking part in an integration scheme can be devised in two ways. It can build upon the basis of national policies and programs, through extensive consultations with national bodies, and pursuing limited objectives in a sequential way so as to upgrade national policy making and forge links among the agencies in the different countries in the region. In this process the national agencies are the protagonists and the staff of the regional organization play a catalytic and supporting role.

The second way in which a common technology policy can be devised is through the regional agency which, after carrying out research, examining other experiences, and assessing the local situation, prepares a common technology policy and a set of programs that are then put forward before the national agencies to obtain their support. There are advantages and disadvantages involved in following either of these approaches. The first may be time-consuming and lead to less coherent technology policy schemes, but it ensures cooperation and facilitates implementation. The second may be faster and lead to a better designed set of policies, but is likely to alienate national agencies and face resistances in the process of implementation, particularly when these national agencies are well established. The choice of one approach or the other, or the relative weight of each in a combined strategy, will depend on the specific context of the integration scheme of which a common technology policy is a part.

The staff of the Andean Common Market chose the second approach, although not without extensive discussions and argumentation within the secretariat. Furthermore, the secretariat initiated an attack on the National Councils for Science and Technology, considering them organizations unsuitable for putting into practice at the national level the provisions contained in the regional technology policy. Regardless of the shortcomings of these organizations, this helped to widen the gap between the national agencies and the secretariat of the Andean Pact, and contributed to a climate of distrust that did not help in the adoption and implementation of the common technology policy.

The provisions contained in the decisions on technology policy have been applied unevenly in the countries of the Andean region. For example, some aspects of Decision 24 on foreign investment and technology transfer were put into effect rather strictly by Peru and Venezuela, but were virtually ignored by Ecuador and Bolivia. Colombia and Chile changed their views radically on Decision 24: though among its supporters in 1970-72, they became its main critics in 1975-76, and in the case of Chile the conflict between national legislation and Decision 24 precipitated its withdrawal from the Andean Pact.

It has been argued that a previous commitment to technological development and to foreign investment control has been the key factor in the application of Decision 24, and Lynn Mytelka suggests that:

. . . Decision 24 was intended, inter alia to facilitate the renegotiation of technology contracts so as to reduce royalty payments, eliminate restrictive clauses and institutionalize procedures for divestment and the

registration of foreign investment. In order to understand the extent to which Decision 24 has indeed accomplished any of these goals, one must examine the
way in which national agencies have chosen to exercise their responsibility. . . . Decision 24 by itself
has had remarkably little direct impact in realizing
these objectives. Domestic legislation which preceded
Decision 24 or which goes beyond Decision 24 and thus
reflects a deeper commitment to the regulation of
direct foreign investment and technology transfer has
been far more effective. [13] (emphasis added)

While this may be true of the regulatory aspects of Decision 24,
mainly because of the existence of professionals and government
agencies with experience in the countries with legislation that preceded Decision 24, this is not the case for Decision 24 as a whole
and for the other decisions on technology policy. For example,
Venezuela--which had no previous legislation on technology policy
and foreign investment regulation--is one of the Andean countries
that has gone farthest in the application of Decision 24.

The approval of Decision 24 provided the basis for the design
of a common technology policy, and the three decisions on Andean
technology development programs (86, 87, and 89) constituted the
first joint efforts for the generation of technology in copper ore
processing and the use of wood from tropical forests. Decision 85,
which contains the common norms regarding industrial property and
is one of the fundamental pillars of a common technology policy, had
not been put into effect three years after it was approved because
the governments of the Andean countries had not made it part of
their national legislation.

In this light, the decisions adopted by the commission of the
Andean Pact on technology policy should be viewed as a structure
around which the real common technology policy will gradually
emerge, one that will allow the Andean countries--once they realize
the importance of a common technology policy for their own development efforts--to transcend the limitations inherent in individual actions for the development of technological capabilities. But the
record on their actual application is mixed, and it is clear that the
commission and the secretariat for the period 1976-78 do not consider technology policy as important and worthy of support as did
the earlier authorities.

Furthermore, the formulation of a common technology policy
establishing common criteria for decision and action is an objective
that can be achieved only in the long term: the different development
models in the countries of the Andean Pact impose constraints and

limitations that cannot be ignored. It is not possible to expect that the technology policy to be followed by one country--a policy that envisages greater social participation in productive activities, the preeminence of the state in certain areas of economic activity, which establishes strict controls on foreign investment, and which is engaged in a series of social and economic transformations--will coincide with the technology policy of another country in which socioeconomic transformations are not given priority, foreign investment is favored as a mechanism for technology transfer, and in which the regulative and productive activities of the state are kept to a minimum.

Nevertheless, in spite of these differences that make it impossible to adopt a common technology policy in the short term in the Andean Pact, there is still a long way to go in the area of joint actions before confronting irreconcilable differences. In the short and medium terms the main task is to initiate a collective learning process and to establish procedures for mutual consultation and exchange of information, to take full advantage of the legal structure available for achieving a greater autonomy of decision in technology matters.

The adoption of common measures in the technology field could also help the Andean Pact in moving away from the periodic crises it has been suffering. There is a limited number of joint sectoral industrial development programs to be developed, and the trade liberalization measures are likely to run into trouble--as has happened with other economic integration schemes among less developed countries. For this reason, and given the success of the Andean technology development programs carried out to date--in terms of actual technical developments, of economic impact, and also in terms of the demonstration effects they have had--it is clear that the Andean integration process would benefit substantially from a greater emphasis on technology matters. Paradoxically, little attention is being paid now to technology policies by the countries and by the secretariat of the Andean Pact. Perhaps a new agency dealing with technology policy independently of the secretariat of the Andean Common Market should be created to take care of these matters.

NOTES

1. See, for example, Gastón Oxman and Francisco Sagasti, La transferencia de tecnología hacia los países del Grupo Andino (Washington, D.C.: Department of Scientific Affairs, OAS, 1972).
2. See Historia Documental del Acuerdo de Cartagena (Lima: Junta del Acuerdo de Cartagena, 1973).
3. For more information on the Andean common technology policies, see Junta del Acuerdo de Cartagena, Andean Pact Technology Policies (Ottawa: IDRC, 1976).

4. For a more detailed diagnosis see Francisco Sagasti and Mauricio Guerrero, El Desarrollo Científico y Tecnológico de América Latina (Buenos Aires: BID/INTAL, 1974), Ch. 1.

5. See Máximo Halty, Producción, Transferencia y Adaptación de Tecnología Industrial (Washington, D.C.: Department of Scientific Affairs, OAS, 1972).

6. Juan C. Gamba, Estadísticas Científico-Tecnológicas de América Latina (Washington, D.C.: Department of Scientific Affairs, OAS, 1972).

7. Amilcar Herrera, Ciencia y Política en América Latina (Mexico City: Siglo XXI Editores, 1971).

8. See Gamba, op. cit.

9. See Pedro L. Díaz, "Análisis Comparativo de los Contratos de Licencia en el Grupo Andino" (Lima: Junta del Acuerdo de Cartagena, 1972), mimeographed; Oxman and Sagasti, op. cit.; and Constantine Vaitsos, Comercialización de tecnología en el Grupo Andino (Lima: Instituto de Estudios Peruanos [IEP], 1973).

10. See ITINTEC, Hacia una política Tecnológica Nacional (Lima: ITINTEC, 1974).

11. See Universidad e Integración Andina, vols. 1 and 2, Santiago de Chile, Corporación de Promoción Universitaria, 1974. Proceedings of an international seminar on the university and Andean integration.

12. For an analysis of the crisis of the Andean Pact see Francisco García Amador, Mauricio Guerrero, and José Nunez del Arco, Grupo Andino: Análisis de una Crisis (Washington, D.C.: Interamerican Development Bank, March 1977).

13. Lynn K. Mytelka, "Direct Foreign Investment, Technology Transfer and Andean Integration," p. 25. In paper presented at the International Political Science Association meeting in Edinburgh, Scotland, August 15-20, 1976.

7

*The ITINTEC System
for Industrial Technology Policy
in Peru*

BACKGROUND TO THE EMERGENCE OF ITINTEC

The awareness of the need to develop national science and technology policies in Peru emerged rather slowly over a period of more
than ten years, although in practice there is still no widespread acceptance that they constitute a legitimate component of the development planning effort. In part this awareness was stirred by external
influence, and in part by the growth and evolution of the scientific
community. Of particular significance were the three seminars organized during 1966-68, at Paracas, El Bosque, and Ancón, where
Peruvian scientists, executives, government officials, and military
personnel met with their North American counterparts and exchanged
ideas on government actions required to stimulate the growth of
science and technology. Several UNESCO missions, staffed mainly
with French experts, also visited the National Planning Institute and
the office of the prime minister, lobbying for the creation of government institutions that would undertake the formulation of national
science and technology policies.

These efforts, and the perseverance of several high-level
scientists and administrators, led to the creation of the Consejo
Nacional de Investigación (National Research Council), in late 1968.
The creation of this body was one of the first pieces of legislation
enacted by the Revolutionary Government of the Armed Forces.
This institution received substantial support from the Regional Program for Scientific and Technological Development of the OAS, and
was able to undertake a series of studies on resources for science

Used with permission from a paper published in <u>World Develop-</u>
<u>ment</u> 3 (November/December 1975): 867-76.

and technology and on transfer of technology. The situation in the late 1960s is revealed to a large extent by these studies.[1] A summary of key facts follows.

The Higher Education System

In 1967 only 14 percent of the students in the higher education system were graduating in scientific or technical disciplines. The great majority, following the Hispanic tradition of colonial times, were being trained in the humanities and law, with a significant percentage in the social sciences. This was in spite of the rapid expansion of the university system. From 1960 to 1970, the number of university students more than tripled, reaching almost 100,000. During this significant increase, the proportion of students in the humanities, including the social sciences, went up from 38 to 47 percent; the relative share of students in education went up from 21 to 24 percent, while the percentage of students in the natural sciences diminished from 8.6 to 4.6 percent. The percentage of engineering students decreased from 20 to 18 percent, while medical students decreased from 12 to 7 percent. The absolute figures present a different picture in the sense that the number of engineering students, for example, doubled during that period. Nevertheless, they indicate that during a phase of rapid expansion of the higher education sector, enrollment in the traditional professions increased faster than in those oriented toward technology.

From nine state universities and one private university in 1960, the number went up to 22 state and 12 private, totaling 34 universities with 253 academic programs and 336 departments (for a student population of less than 100,000). Clearly, it was almost impossible to maintain high standards in an expansion process of this kind.

In 1970 the university system in Peru spent approximately 1.8 percent of its total budget on research, amounting to U.S. $1.5 million. However, many administrative and teaching tasks were allocated to the research budgets and a significant proportion was devoted to agricultural research in state-run experimentation stations attached to the universities. On average, less than U.S. $60,000 per year were spent by each university for research, and about U.S. $15 per year per student. These average figures hide wide disparities, for most of the research budgets were concentrated in half a dozen state universities and three or four private institutions.

To complete the picture on higher education, it is also known that about 15 percent of engineers who graduated between 1962 and 1966 emigrated to the United States, Canada, and France, while a smaller percentage from the natural and social sciences and medicine, together amounting to about 9 percent, also did so. These figures indicate the lack of a solid basis of highly trained manpower on which to develop an indigenous capacity for the generation of technology. If the statistics on scientific and technological activities are examined, the outlook is confirmed.

In effect, according to surveys and estimates made in 1970 by the National Research Council, there were 184 research institutions in Peru, employing a total of 2,900 workers. Of these, less than one-half belonged to the category of researchers and technicians, and even less worked full time in research tasks. Most of this personnel was involved in natural and exact sciences (29 percent), in agriculture (28 percent), in the medical sciences (21 percent), with only 10 percent working in the engineering field (the rest being in the social sciences). A total of about U.S. $5.9 million was allocated for current research expenditures in 1970, with a substantially smaller amount allocated to investment expenditures. Allowing for omissions and capital investments, the total is certain not to exceed U.S. $10 million.

Turning now to average ratios, these figures imply that there were less than 16 workers--and even fewer researchers--per institution, that each institution spent around U.S. $32,100 per year, and that each worker was allocated about U.S. $2,000 per year. Additional data show that the number of research projects under way exceeded 1,100, which would imply an average of 1.7 workers per project and an average allocation of U.S. $5,200 per year per project.

All of this gives the picture of a rather small and fragmented research system, requiring a process of concentration and rationalization, a significant influx of funds, and a substantial increase in the number of researchers. However, it must also be pointed out that engineering training in the mid-1960s, particularly at the National Engineering University, had achieved rather high standards, and that there were many professionals and scientists struggling to do research under very adverse conditions. A few "pockets" were created, most notably in genetics, geophysics, medicine, theoretical physics, anthropology, mathematics, development economics, and a few other subjects. These groups managed by various means to survive and do high-quality work.

The situation with regard to the transfer of technology has been widely studied in several reports. [2] Here it will suffice to say that the transfer of technology in Peru, particularly via licensing agreements, had most of the defects and showed most of the abuses that have been often documented. It was clear that the importation of foreign technology did not contribute effectively to the development of indigenous technical capabilities in industry, and even less to the development of an autonomous capacity for decision making in matters of technology. Also the economic environment and the cumulative effect of past policies promoting import substitution were very clearly felt. Elsewhere a description of the technological effects of some characteristics of the economic system, and of government economic policies for Latin American countries in general, has been given.[3] These apply rather well to the Peruvian situation, for in the late 1960s the first phases of the easy import substitution process were being exhausted.

Legal and Government Measures

The changes initiated and sustained by the Revolutionary Government of the Armed Forces have modified this situation at a fast, although uneven, pace. After the creation of the National Research Council, which has been mostly ineffective and almost a handicap to technological development, the General Law of Industries, passed in July of 1970, was the next landmark in the evolution of a policy for the development of technical capabilities in industry. Among the significant measures introduced by this law, it is worthwhile to single out a transition from the policy of import substitution industrialization, which sought to exploit backward linkages from consumer goods and light durables to intermediate and basic industry, to a policy of industrialization based on the development of basic and capital goods industries that would have both forward linkage effects (through the production of inputs for intermediate and consumer industries), and backward linkage effects (through a more intensive use of national resources). The law also sanctioned greater participation of the state in the industrialization process, not only in a promotional role, but also through entrepreneurial activities, particularly in the basic industries. With regard to ownership, the law established a system of workers' participation through the industrial community, a collective entity grouping all workers in each enterprise, which, by using a certain percentage of net income, will gradually acquire shares and hence the right to participate in the administration and management of the enterprise. In relation to ownership, the law also stipulates the gradual transformation of foreign into mixed and national enterprises, setting limits on the percentage of foreign capital. Finally, the law establishes a system of incentives based on the priority assigned to products. Those assigned first priority are given incentives (reduction of import duties, tax exemptions on reinvestments, special credit conditions, and so on) in greater proportion than those in second or third priority.

The General Law of Industries also has several articles dealing specifically with technology matters. Two of these, Articles 14 and 15, refer to the creation of ITINTEC and to the industrial technology research fund formed by allocating 2 percent of the net income of industrial enterprises before taxes. These two articles constitute the foundation on which the ITINTEC system of industrial research was created. There is also a clause stating that the enterprises that produce technology will be given first-priority treatment with regard to incentives. In addition to the ITINTEC system, the general laws of mining, fisheries, and telecommunications contain similar clauses that direct 2 percent of net income before taxes (1 percent in the case of mining) to technological research. Unlike the case of ITINTEC, where enterprises have the first option to use the funds they generate, in these cases the money goes to a central fund. Also, during the past four years the allocations to agricultural research, health research, to marine sciences, and to science and technology in general have grown considerably, changing rather drastically the picture shown earlier for 1970.

In the area of technology transfer, Peru has created a structure of National Registry Offices (Organismos Nacionales Competentes) according to the stipulations of Decision 24 of the Andean Pact Commission. This has involved the creation of a registry of licensing agreements, changes in the organization of the industrial property office, the creation of a committee to oversee foreign investment, and the transformation of foreign enterprises into mixed or local ownership, and the installation of a consultation process to screen technologies to be imported.

Summarizing the background at the time ITINTEC became active in the early 1970s, it is possible to characterize the situation as follows:

Emergence of sectoral institutions under the aegis of ministries (industry, mining, telecommunications, and the like), with stable sources of funds derived from a percentage of the net income of enterprises in the sector, and which have the mission of programming, financing, and carrying out technological research and training. The amount of funds made available through these institutions may exceed 1,000 million Peruvian soles per year (approximately U.S. $25 million) by the mid-1970s. In consequence they now become the key institutions with regard to technology policy.

Incapacity of the National Research Council--or for that matter of any central agency--to carry out the task of devising science and technology policies for the whole country. In consequence, the council is structurally unable to perform the functions assigned to it by law, which were defined at a time when the confusion between science policy and technology policy was the rule. If the council is to be effective, it must reorient its activities toward the promotion of scientific research, leaving the functions of formulating and implementing technology policies to the sectoral institutions that are better suited to do so. This does not imply that intersectoral coordination is not necessary, but rather that there are better mechanisms (for example an interministerial committee) for coordinating the technology policies of different sectors.

Continuing isolation of the university research system from national needs. This is partly a reflection of the crisis through which the Peruvian university is passing, although the resources that could be channeled through the sectoral funds may revitalize research in the university (provided that it is transferred to it primarily through contractual agreements). This could reduce substantially the isolation of research in universities.

Initiation of the mechanisms for controlling the imports of technology, which will require substantial development before they become fully operative.

The increased sources of funds, and the orientation and training programs instituted by the sectoral agencies in charge of technology policy, have also had the effect of increasing the availability of manpower for research tasks. Although the lack of high-level scientists, technicians, and professionals to conceive and lead research projects constitutes perhaps the major bottleneck in the system, there appears to be a hidden capacity to identify, formulate, and carry out research projects, both in industry and the university, so that the shortage of qualified manpower has not proved to be as critical as was once thought.

BASIC FEATURES OF THE ITINTEC SYSTEM

Two years after the General Law of Industries established the basis for the creation of ITINTEC, the Organic Law of the institution was approved. This law established the objectives, structure, and operational mechanisms through which the ITINTEC system functions. The board of directors was constituted toward the end of 1972 and, after one year of transition during which most of the general policies were laid out, a new management, under the direction of Isaás Flit, took over and has been running ITINTEC ever since. Since its creation the board has been working closely with ITINTEC executives to design the policies and policy instruments that will enable the institution to fulfill its functions.

The ITINTEC system is an attempt to deal comprehensively with the problems of industrial technology policy in an underdeveloped country. It is a multiple-function organization that operates several policy instruments to develop technological capabilities in Peruvian industry.[4] (See Chapter 5.) The Organic Law of ITINTEC assigned the functions of promoting, supervising, and carrying out industrial technological research; of preparing national technical norms and standards and improving quality control in industry; and of performing additional activities such as providing technical information for industry. As a result of the reorganization of the Ministry of Industry and Tourism in late 1974, the functions of providing technical information, documentation, and extension services for industry were expanded, and the functions of dealing with industrial property and of negotiating and registering licensing agreements were transferred to ITINTEC. During the years of operation of ITINTEC the board of directors has also defined complementary fields for action covering areas such as engineering and industrial design, export of technology, training of personnel for technological research, and the formulation of industrial technology policies. Furthermore, ITINTEC has also developed very close working relationships with other organizations in the industrial sector and with institutions that perform functions similar to those of ITINTEC in other sectors. In sum, ITINTEC has become the executive agency for the formulation and implementation of industrial technology policy in Peru. This chapter will cover only the activities related to industrial research, although before doing so it is necessary to describe a few general principles established by the board which govern the functions of ITINTEC.

In the first place ITINTEC will use the existing capacity for technological research in enterprises, universities, and research institutions to the fullest possible extent, seeking to turn them into centers for the generation of technology. Of particular importance are the technical capabilities of industry, which have lain dormant for many years, and which could be directed toward the identification of technical problems that require systematic and imaginative solution. This implies a belief in the existence of a hidden capacity for technological research, which should be uncovered and used to enhance the technical level of Peruvian industry.

Second, in accordance with the National Development Plan, ITINTEC will decentralize its activities, establishing a nationwide network of entities for the generation of technology. This implies not only spreading funds for research throughout the country, but also locating technology centers in various parts of the country to perform technical activities to support industry, both in the region where the center is located and at the national level.

Third, the promotion of a demand for local technology is one of the key principles that orient the operations of ITINTEC. This is done through the involvement, right from the beginning, of the users of the results in the formulation of technological research projects, and by forging links between users and producers of technological knowledge. This is of particular importance in the case of industrial enterprises that have remained relatively isolated from the development of technology research institutions until now. Also, the organization of a system by means of which a certain proportion of an enterprise's net income must be spent on research generates an incentive for the enterprise to look at its technical problems more closely, and hence an increased demand for local technology and technological services.

Other principles that govern the activity of ITINTEC include the need to intervene directly and actively in the process of importation of technology, seeking to link this process with the production of domestic technology. Given that the great majority of the technology used by industry comes from abroad, this activity is of great importance for the definition of research projects that will enable the enterprises to adapt, modify, and absorb the imported technologies. This will lead to a progressive participation of local technological institutions in the evaluation of imported technology, the disaggregation of the technological package, and the selection of the technologies most appropriate to specific conditions in the country. Also, whenever possible ITINTEC will seek to provide direct assistance to small- and medium-scale enterprises that lack the technical personnel to perform research tasks.

Perforce, ITINTEC will have to function as an invisible university for training personnel for industrial technological research. Enterprises and institutions carrying out research projects within the ITINTEC system are encouraged to include students from the universities in their projects so that they participate actively in the research project and learn while doing. This also implies the need for acting as an agent to relate high-level specialized professionals with industries that may require their services for a specific problem.

Finally, given the magnitude of the task involved and the dangers of growing too fast, ITINTEC will expand its activities gradually, carefully balancing short-term achievements with long-term objectives. ITINTEC will also avoid excessive growth with a centralized management structure, and it may eventually turn into a conglomerate, which covers a variety of activities related to industrial technology policy. In that sense what is sought is a balance between comprehensiveness in the formulation and implementation of industrial technology policies, and the efficiency of a small organization with specific functions to perform.

INDUSTRIAL TECHNOLOGICAL RESEARCH IN ITINTEC

An underdeveloped country has to give the concept of research the content that fits its own situation. In the Peruvian case, Isaías

Flit, the director general of ITINTEC, has defined industrial technological research as the application of imagination with scientific
rigor to the solution of a concrete technical problem in industry.
In this way, the spectrum of technological activities covered is
greatly expanded, and the usual discussions on applied versus basic
research are avoided. For example, if the solution of a concrete
technical problem in industry required the performance of research
tasks of a fundamental nature, they would be included within the
scope of ITINTEC. This definition also puts emphasis on the source
of research projects, namely the concrete technical problems of industry, and on the two key components of research: imagination and
scientific rigor.

Bearing this definition in mind, it is possible to understand
better the orientation of industrial research activities of ITINTEC.
Figure 7.1 summarizes the way in which funds can be used within
the ITINTEC system of industrial technological research. Every
industrial enterprise is required to put aside for the performance of
technological research 2 percent of its net income before taxes.
The enterprise has the first option to use the funds if it decides to
present a research project and ITINTEC approves it. The enterprise can perform the research on its own premises if it has the
manpower and equipment necessary, or it can contract out the research to some other entity (primarily universities). In this case
the enterprise and the research center sign an agreement whose general terms and conditions are specified by ITINTEC in a model contract. If the enterprise decides not to present a research project,
or if the project presented is not approved, then the 2 percent of net
income before taxes has to be deposited at the National Bank in a
special account in the name of the research fund of ITINTEC.

With the funds gathered from enterprises that do not present
projects, or whose projects are rejected, ITINTEC can carry out its
own projects, contract out projects with universities and other centers, or subsidize research projects that are being carried out by
enterprises. In this latter case, preference is given to enterprises
undertaking joint research in collaboration with others, and to medium
and small enterprises that have worthwhile research projects but
whose funds are not sufficient.

To guide enterprises in the formulation of research projects,
ITINTEC has prepared a manual specifying the structure and content
of the proposals to be presented by industries, universities, or any
other entities. The proposals go through an evaluation process by
the technical staff and, depending on the amount of funds involved,
they are either approved by the director general or by the board of
ITINTEC. In addition to requesting research projects from the enterprises, ITINTEC also asks individual researchers and research

FIGURE 7.1

Uses of ITINTEC's Research Fund

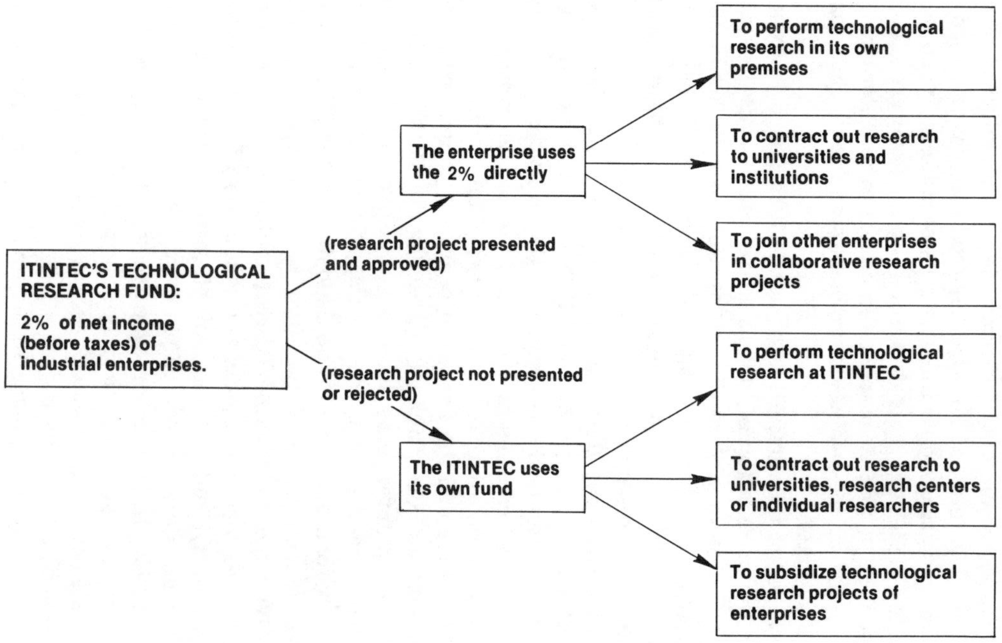

ITINTEC'S TECHNOLOGICAL RESEARCH FUND:

2% of net income (before taxes) of industrial enterprises.

(research project presented and approved)

(research project not presented or rejected)

The enterprise uses the 2% directly

The ITINTEC uses its own fund

To perform technological research in its own premises

To contract out research to universities and institutions

To join other enterprises in collaborative research projects

To perform technological research at ITINTEC

To contract out research to universities, research centers or individual researchers

To subsidize technological research projects of enterprises

Source: Constructed by the author.

126

organizations to submit proposals that could be financed out of
ITINTEC's fund. Once a project is approved, a contract is signed
between ITINTEC and the entity that will carry it out. It specifies
the terms and conditions of the agreement, establishes a detailed
program of expenditures, and defines reporting procedures. The
projects are monitored by ITINTEC's technical staff, the progress
of the project followed, and final results evaluated upon completion.

ITINTEC's direct research activities had not been fully implemented in 1976, and there was a plan for creating several technology
centers throughout the country, in which ITINTEC would carry out
its own projects. An intermediate solution was also considered, by
means of which ITINTEC personnel would use the equipment of other
organizations or enterprises to do research.

Development of Industrial Technological
Capabilities in Underdeveloped Countries

The system outlined in the preceding paragraphs has several
characteristics that make it rather interesting for the purpose of
promoting the development of industrial technological capabilities in
underdeveloped countries. First, it provides a protected market
for research and development. By specifying that funds can be used
only to finance research projects (and by making ITINTEC the guar-
antor that funds are used for this sole purpose) it generates an effective demand for technological research. Given that enterprises face
the option of using the funds for technological research or turning
them over to ITINTEC, there is an incentive to examine the technological problems of the enterprise. If the management is already
convinced of the value of research, this will be seen as an additional
encouragement; and if management is indifferent to technological
problems, this may generate a concern for improving technical
capabilities.

Second, a decentralized system is established whereby the
definition of research projects is spread throughout industry, avoiding excessive centralization in the definition of research priorities
and projects. The presumption is that industrial enterprises know
better than anybody else their own problems and are able to formulate research projects that truly respond to their own technological
needs. Together with the guidelines for the preparation and presentation of projects, enterprises are further informed, through a set
of criteria, as to what constitutes a worthwhile project from the
point of view of ITINTEC. During the phases preceding the formal
presentation, and sometimes even after this, there is a continuous
dialogue between ITINTEC staff and enterprise management, in order

to arrive at the definition of a research project that could be approved by ITINTEC. The main concern is to give enterprises as much assistance as possible so that they can develop their own capacity for the identification, preparation, and execution of research projects or, alternatively, to develop their own capacity for identifying and defining terms of reference so that the projects can be carried out by specialized research agencies. All of this implies that the basis for the activities of ITINTEC is the research project, and that wide-ranging, open-ended programs, preliminary ideas, and unstructured research programs with no clear contribution to enterprise and national objectives are not accepted. The performance of technological research projects, or the capacity for specifying terms of reference for other entities, would lead to an increase in the technology absorption capacity of industry. To allow for projects that last more than one year, the ITINTEC system provides that an enterprise can allocate its 2 percent for up to five consecutive years for the realization of a particular project.

Contract Research

Central to the operation of the ITINTEC research system is the concept that contractual arrangements should be used for specific projects, rather than grant subsidies or allocate funds to open-ended research projects. The idea is to develop the habit of contract research by making enterprises pay for a specific service, and therefore become concerned about the results they get. On the other hand, this also forces the research institutions to deliver the goods in accordance with the objectives, terms, and conditions specified in the research project and the contract. This is of particular importance in view of the fact that the 2 percent system provides a stable source of funds, free from budgetary negotiations, which could perpetuate a situation where irrelevant research is supported indefinitely.

State Participation

Another key characteristic of the ITINTEC system is that the state participates actively in the support of industrial research on a decentralized basis. In effect, the 2 percent is computed before taxes and therefore the state is foregoing the income it would have obtained if the 2 percent were computed after taxes. In some cases, for relatively large enterprises, this could reach almost one-half of the 2 percent. Together with this financial support, there is the right of the state to participate in the use of equipment and materials and in the results generated by the projects. To this end, ITINTEC follows the policy of avoiding the duplication of expensive research equipment by orienting research projects of the same type to a particular center, or by asking that equipment be put at the disposal of other enterprises or research centers that require it. ITINTEC carries an inventory of equipment purchased with the 2 percent fund as a means of putting this policy into practice.

Ownership of Results

The situation is more complicated with regard to the ownership of results (primarily patents), and in this respect ITINTEC has followed a very flexible policy, treating each research project on its own merits. Clearly, there may be some instances in which enterprises that have obtained worthwhile results should derive some advantage over their competitors; but on the other hand, there may be cases in which the knowledge produced is of too great importance to be used by one entity alone, particularly in research projects carried out by universities and specialized research institutions. This issue also has implications with regard to the financial returns to the results of research activities, and here again ITINTEC follows a flexible policy, so that royalties may be shared in various proportions by ITINTEC and the entities carrying out the research.

Priorities of Research Projects

The existence of a research fund directly at the disposal of ITINTEC provides the institution with the opportunity to reallocate funds for technological research in accordance with the needs of industrial development. In particular, it allows ITINTEC to fill the gaps when existing enterprises do not carry out technological research activities. In this respect ITINTEC has developed, in close coordination with the sectoral planning office of the Ministry of Industry and Tourism, approximately 50 profiles of research projects on which proposals have been requested from universities and research centers. These projects refer to natural resources available in the country, to areas where new investments are planned, to specific problems that require urgent solutions, and to the development of research projects necessary to provide a technical infrastructure for industry as a whole.

The ITINTEC system of industrial technological research provides for widespread inputs into the process of defining priorities for industrial research. The sources of priorities and of research projects in ITINTEC are the following: projects presented by enterprises, which respond to their specific technical needs; projects developed jointly with the sectoral planning office of the Ministry of Industry and Tourism, or with the planning offices of other ministries, which respond to the needs of national development; proposals by universities, research institutes, or individual researchers, which respond to the opportunities that they see to exploit economically a particular line of research; projects that arise out of specific short-run problems and that must be solved rapidly by a contingency technology research project, such as specific demands of government agencies as a result of urgent problems; projects that emerge out of ITINTEC's own planning effort, which respond to anticipated technological problems in areas where ITINTEC must intervene; projects arising out of anticipated technological problems that international commitments may impose on Peruvian industry, such as the case of industrial programming in the Andean Pact; and projects arising out of basic research results that show an economic potential for their application.

This scheme ensures diversification of the sources of research proposals and of research priorities. It is ITINTEC's task, and particularly that of its board of directors and director general, to harmonize and consolidate projects arising out of these sources into a coherent whole, with the aims of attaining the objectives of developing technological capabilities in industry and of acquiring a capacity for autonomous decision making in matters of technology.

A PRELIMINARY APPRAISAL OF THE ITINTEC SYSTEM

In the first stage of the development of ITINTEC (between the General Law of Industries in the middle of 1970 and the time the new administration took over in late 1973) a total of 108 projects were submitted by enterprises, even in the absence of guidelines from ITINTEC. Of these, 54 were approved and most of them were completed by 1975. In addition, three large research projects were generated by ITINTEC and contracted out to universities. These preliminary projects showed that it was feasible to operate the ITINTEC research system and pointed out several problems and deficiencies that are being corrected.

Research Projects Generated

The first organized drive to generate research projects by industry and to develop ITINTEC's own portfolio of projects began in late 1973. The manual for the preparation and submission of research projects was published and given wide dissemination in January 1974, and the deadline for presenting research proposals was April 1. Response was enthusiastic, aided by several seminars conducted by ITINTEC's staff and board members, and with the participation of the minister of industry and tourism. A total of 189 project proposals were presented, amounting approximately to 350 million soles (approximately U.S. $8.6 million). Industrial enterprises presented 160 projects for a total of 318 million soles, 27 projects were presented by research centers for a total of 30 million soles, and two other projects were presented by individual researchers. The projects were distributed by field as shown in Table 7.1, the majority being in the food-processing and tobacco industries.*

Of the 160 projects presented by enterprises, 12 were withdrawn and 89 were approved by ITINTEC, corresponding to approximately 142 million soles. The procedure established for approvals gave the director general discretionary power over projects, or groups of projects, that did not exceed 1.5 million soles, the rest being approved by the board of directors. Table 7.1 gives a breakdown of the projects that were actually approved. For practically all of these, the respective contracts were signed and the research tasks begun by 1975. The average lifetime of a project is about 21 months, although there are wide variations.

It is still too early to evaluate how these projects were carried out and whether the results obtained justify the investment. However, given the lack of research tradition in Peruvian industry, ITINTEC views the projects of the first few years as part of a learning process in which both the enterprises and ITINTEC will learn from their own experiences and from each other. In this sense, certain inefficiencies and mistakes must be tolerated in the early projects carried out by a particular enterprise. Through this process ITINTEC will also find out the type of assistance needed by industry and will be able to orient its technical services in this direction.† The process of monitoring the research projects under way has already begun, and early findings confirm, as did the first group of 54 projects, that the hidden capacity for technological research can be made effective for the

---

*For the 1975 campaign, 91 projects had been presented by April 30 for a total of 314 million soles. About 90 percent of these projects were presented by industrial enterprises.

†Since ITINTEC's establishment approximately 300 different enterprises have submitted research projects. Of these, about 100 enterprises have presented projects more than once.

TABLE 7.1

Industrial Technological Research Projects, 1974

	Projects Presented		Projects Authorized			
Project Areas	Number	Percentage of Total	Number	Percentage of Total	Project Cost (thousands of soles)	Percentage of Total Cost
Food, beverages, and tobacco	42	26.3	20	22.5	32,414	22.8
Textiles	15	9.4	11	12.4	12,456	8.8
Pharmaceutics and cosmetics	3	1.9	1	1.1	152	0.1
Metals working	28	17.5	20	22.5	53,563	37.7
Rubber, leather, and plastics	12	7.5	10	11.2	15,133	10.7
Wood and cellulose products	4	2.5	2	2.2	2,087	1.5
Chemical products	19	11.9	11	12.4	10,725	7.5
Nonmetallic mineral products	14	8.7	7	7.9	9,189	6.5
Machinery, equipment, and electric and electronic products	9	5.6	4	4.5	5,287	3.7
Miscellaneous	14	8.7	3	3.3	1,059	0.7
Total	160	100.0	89	100.0	142,065	100.0

Source: ITINTEC: La investigación tecnológica industrial en el Perú, Lima, 1975.

132

performance of technological activities of direct relevance to industrial needs.

With regard to ITINTEC's own research portfolio, through a process of consultation with the planning office of the Ministry of Industry and Tourism and through discussions with the research community, a total of 48 project profiles were identified. These profiles describe the objectives of the research, its main characteristics, and give rough estimates of manpower needs, time required for completion, and total cost. The project profiles were distributed to research institutions and specific proposals were requested from them. The rate of response was satisfactory, and a few months after the profiles were circulated among the research community, more than 25 proposals were received, the majority from university research centers.

Once the system is stabilized, it is expected that approximately 100 research projects will be presented to ITINTEC every year, and that about 20 projects will be defined and carried out by ITINTEC. The latter should increase once the technology centers become operational. It is also expected that, as the learning process goes on, a smaller number of projects will be rejected.

This raises the question of the absorption capacity of the industrial research community to cope with a tenfold increase in available funds compared to the level of 1970. In this respect, it is important to recall the definition of research given at the beginning of the preceding section. If the traditional concept of industrial technological research is maintained, it is clear that the high-level manpower needed to direct the projects will take time to develop. If the wider definition--more in accordance with our present technological situation--is accepted, there are a large number of professionals who can participate actively in the system. In conjunction with the training activities of ITINTEC and with the learning effects of carrying out research projects, it is expected that the shortage of qualified manpower will not become the acute bottleneck that it may appear to be at first.

Problems and Deficiencies

Several problem areas have emerged that merit some attention in this preliminary evaluation. First, the work involved in establishing a system of the nature and magnitude of ITINTEC imposes great strain on the administrative and political capabilities of the executives. The core group of trained professionals who took up policy and administrative positions in ITINTEC were under great pressure from several fronts. Part of the professional staff of the organization found it difficult to become accustomed to the philosophy and rhythm of the work imposed. However, a remarkable degree of cohesion was achieved among the professionals and it was not unusual to see them working late and devoting their spare time to ITINTEC-related activities, which is not common in institutions in the public sector. Pressures to provide technical assistance were also felt from enterprises, and there were pressures from the government bureaucracy which found it difficult to accept the flexible ways in which ITINTEC operated.

A second difficulty, which is inherent in the fixed 2 percent allocation, is that there is a bias in favor of the relatively large enterprises whose research funds exceed the minimal critical volume required to support a research team. There are several possible solutions to this bias, and the policy has been to use the funds at the disposal of ITINTEC to offset this imbalance. Other solutions, such as graduating the level of the allocation according to the size of net income, would be too cumbersome to operate.

In terms of the formulation and presentation of research projects, difficulties have emerged in the efforts to introduce the concept of contract research, with the project as the basic unit of analysis. This requires an educational process and continuous dialogue with ITINTEC's technical staff. The demands imposed by this consultation process have been heavy and rather difficult to handle with the relatively small number of professionals (about 40) who work in the Technology Division. On the other hand, a rapid expansion of professional staff would not permit maintenance of the conceptual orientation and cohesion that are necessary to disseminate ITINTEC's philosophy of industrial technological research. This also has implications for project monitoring.

Serious problems with regard to the property of results and to the use of equipment purchased with the 2 percent funds have not arisen as yet, although the relevant policies for dealing with a variety of situations are now under consideration.

The need to implement as soon as possible a network of technology centers that will enable ITINTEC to perform its own research activities and provide services to industry is being examined closely. Feasibility studies are now under way for the establishment of at least four technology centers throughout the country, and it is expected that the first will start operations in 1978. Parallel with the feasibility studies is a search for highly trained personnel to staff the centers.

CONCLUSION

This chapter has presented a Peruvian case study of the formulation and implementation of industrial technology policies, through the development of ITINTEC. It is necessary to stress that the study presents only a partial view of ITINTEC. It does not cover activities related to technical norms and standards, quality control, licensing agreements, industrial property, information and extension services, industrial design, and so on. Some of these have been fully implemented, some are now under way, and others are at the policy formulation stage. Nevertheless, they constitute, from the point of view of ITINTEC, a coherent whole on which action will be taken when the time comes within the framework of a long-range institutional development plan.

NOTES

1. See, for example, Potencial Científico y Tecnológico del Perú, Consejo Nacional de Investigación (Lima, 1974).

2. See, for instance, a series of eight sectoral reports on technology transfer published by the Consejo Nacional de Investigación between 1971 and 1974. A summary of early data appears in Gastón Oxman and Francisco Sagasti, La Transferencia de Tecnología hacia los Países del Grupo Andino (Washington, D.C.: Department of Scientific Affairs, OAS, 1972).

3. Francisco Sagasti and Mauricio Guerrero, El Desarrollo Científico y Tecnológico de América Latina (Buenos Aires: BID/INTAL, 1974).

4. For a general overview of the lines of action for technology policy followed by ITINTEC, see Hacia una Política Tecnológica Nacional (Lima: ITINTEC, 1974); Isaías Flit, El Conocimiento, Base Común de la Generación y Transferencia de Tecnología (Lima: ITINTEC, 1974).

8

The Role of the University in Scientific and Technological Development

INSTITUTIONAL FRAMEWORK FOR THE DEVELOPMENT OF SCIENCE AND TECHNOLOGY

The establishment of an adequate institutional infrastructure is one of the necessary preconditions for autonomous scientific and technological development. This infrastructure comprises organizations, legal frameworks, and explicit and implicit norms to regulate the interactions among the actors involved in science and technology.

In order to appreciate the role that the university can play in the process of scientific and technological development, it is necessary to consider first the broad range of institutions that intervene in the process of generating, modifying, distributing, and utilizing knowledge. In general it is possible to distinguish three categories of institutions: those that fulfill central guidance and orientation functions; those engaged in the actual performance of scientific and technological activities; and those that perform a linkage function with institutions and organizations in other spheres of socioeconomic activities. The first provide general policy guidelines, coordinate the performance of activities, and carry out promotional tasks. The second perform scientific and technological activities that generate and modify the flows of knowledge, as well as activities that permit these flows to reach the users of such knowledge. The third group of institutions has the function of linking those in the second group

Used with permission from a contribution to the volume: Corporación de Promoción Universitaria (CPU), La Universidad Latinoamericana y el Avance Científico-Tecnológico (Santiago de Chile: 1974).

with the users of scientific and technical knowledge, and also that of relating them with the suppliers of human, financial, and physical resources.

Table 8.1 contains an illustrative list of the institutions comprised in each of the three categories. It indicates only the range of possible organizations involved in the generation, modification, and distribution of knowledge, and in the orientation of scientific and technological activities. From this list it can be appreciated that the university is only one among the many institutions that participate in the science and technology system, and that in principle there is no reason for it to play the dominant role.

TABLE 8.1

Functions in the Scientific and Technological System
Performed by Various Institutions

Central Guidance Functions
  Policy Making and Planning
    Ministries of science and technology
    National councils for science and technology
    Cabinet level advisory committees
    National offices for science and technology
    National research councils
  Coordination and Promotion
    National academies of science
    Various other national academies (medicine, engineering)
    Associations for the advancement of science
    National Funds for research and development
    Various professional associations
    Foundations (local and foreign)

Operating Functions
  Carrying Out Scientific and Technological Activities
    Universities
    Research and development institutes
    National laboratories
    Cooperative research associations
    Research divisions of various government dependencies
    Industrial firms (local and foreign)
    Industrial research and development centers
    Academies of science

(continued)

Table 8.1, continued

Providing Support and Services
  National laboratories
  Information and documentation centers
  Survey organizations (natural resources, social sciences, etc.)
  Astronomical and meteorological observatories
  Technical norms and specifications institutes
  Museums
  Productivity centers
  Patent offices
  Organizations to control the import of technology

Interface Functions
  Relating the Producers and Users of Knowledge
    Engineering design organizations
    Banks and other organizations that provide capital for new
      technology ventures
    Specialized consulting firms
    Extension services
  Relating the System with the Sources of Qualified Manpower
    Universities
    Fellowship programs and organizations
    Specialized training institutions
    Technical assistance organizations

Source: Compiled by the author.

INSTITUTIONS INVOLVED IN THE PRODUCTION AND MODIFICATION OF KNOWLEDGE

The activities of production and modification of knowledge constitute the central axis around which an autonomous scientific and technological capacity is developed. In principle it is possible to identify five types of organizational units that carry out these activities: educational research units, basic research units, applied or action-oriented research units, research units in enterprises and other users of knowledge, and units for popular participation in research tasks. This typology is based on functional criteria and does not necessarily imply an institutional setting. For example, a basic research unit can be located at a university or in a government dependency, or it can be autonomous. Similarly, an educational research unit need not be located at a university, for there are independent organizations that can simultaneously perform teaching and research functions.

Educational Research Units

The basic postulate for an educational research unit is that teaching and the preparation of professionals and scientists have priority over research tasks. Its mission is to prepare qualified human resources, for which the active participation in research and development is used as a pedagogical instrument. This type of unit should put in practice the principle that the most effective way of acquiring knowledge is to participate actively in scientific and technological research activities, under the guidance of a more experienced teacher or tutor.

Two modes of action can be distinguished for educational research units. First, there are educational research units associated with undergraduate education. Here the idea is to imbue the students with a critical attitude and to put within their reach the basic principles of the scientific method through their application in concrete situations. The research associated with undergraduate education should be only a means to prepare the professionals who are to contribute to the country's development effort, and should not be considered an end in itself. For this reason it is convenient to put emphasis on social science research, which serves a dual purpose: to familiarize the students with the scientific method, and also to make them aware of the social processes around them.

Second, there are the educational research units associated with postgraduate education. The human resources on which the scientific and technological system can count come, with very few exceptions, from the university centers of graduate education. The research tasks should cover a large variety of fields, from curiosity-oriented research of the fundamental kind, all the way to highly specific research programs that may help in the solution of concrete problems. The central emphasis in this type of unit is the preparation of highly qualified personnel, using the research programs and the participation of graduate students in them as means to achieve this.

The first modality can be put in practice through research projects in the social sciences (sociology, economics, anthropology, and so on), in which the students are involved in the gathering, processing, and analysis of data under the direction of a professor. In addition to learning while doing research, the students can contribute to a greater knowledge of the social reality of their country. It is also possible to organize multidisciplinary groups of students to undertake concrete tasks in fields such as agriculture, water resources, mineral resources, and the like in remote areas of the country about which little is known. These multidisciplinary groups of students can provide limited technical assistance to the inhabitants of these zones and help to identify more serious problems that escape their competence. A program of this type was put into practice in Peru in the mid-1960s under the name of Cooperación Popular.

The second modality is put into practice through graduate research centers in universities, about which there is already a tradition in Latin America, primarily because the majority of scientific and technological research has been conducted in university centers with the participation of graduate students.

Basic Research Units

The main principle that governs the functioning of basic research units is to award priority to the generation of knowledge in the widest possible sense, but also to consider the country's long-term needs for scientific and technological knowledge. The preparation of qualified researchers in these units is a by-product of the generation of knowledge. The areas covered by this type of unit should be conditioned by the long-term vision of the future of the country, by the needs for knowledge generated within the science and technology system, and by the need to act as a link between the local scientific community and international efforts in science and technology.

In the first case the idea is to identify problem areas whose solution requires counting on an indigenous scientific capacity. For example, if the long-term development strategy envisages the intensive use of marine resources, it will be necessary to do basic research on marine biology, consumption habits for marine products, the existence of sea-bed mineral resources, the behavior of marine currents, and so on. If the development pattern foresees considerable urban growth, it will be necessary to do research on rural-urban migration, on the possible structure of employment and the way of increasing it, and on the changes in attitudes and values that arise from massive urbanization. This will help in linking the growth of scientific and technological capabilities with the development path envisaged for the country.

The second group of themes for the research to be performed by these units arises from the needs for basic knowledge of other institutions in the scientific and technological system. For example, some applied research programs in metallurgy may require fundamental research in the area of solid-state physics, and a basic research unit can act as a resource at the disposal of units requiring this service. In the case of social sciences, it is possible that anthropological and sociological studies may require basic knowledge in mathematics (for example, graph theory).

Finally, the research themes derived from the need to link the local scientific community with the advances of science on a world scale will depend on the structure of the scientific and technological activities in the country. For example, in the case of nuclear research, and in the absence of a strong base of scientific and technological activities in this area, a basic research unit can carry out theoretical investigations that will help in appreciating and understanding the progress of the international scientific community in nuclear matters. A secondary effect of the activity of this type of unit is to prepare highly qualified scientific personnel through their participation in research.

Applied or Action-Oriented Research Units

The main function of applied research units is to provide the knowledge required for the social and economic activities directly related to the process of development. The themes for research emerge out of problems that have no existing answers or guidelines for their solution. These problem areas arise in the social, physical, and natural sciences and cover a variety of fields ranging from the improvement of public administration, to the use of unexploited resources, and to the prevention of diseases.

Two subsidiary functions of this type of center are to prepare qualified personnel to direct applied research programs and to retrain professionals, updating their knowledge base through their participation in research programs. Another function of this type of unit is to intervene actively in the process of technology transfer, seeking the most effective way of absorbing and making permanent the imported knowledge.

This type of unit should fill the void existing between the production of basic or potentially useful knowledge--whether generated by the two preceding types of units or imported from abroad--and the scientific and technological activities that put technical knowledge directly at the disposal of the user. However, the idea is not to perform consulting activities or routine tasks. This type of unit should not undertake the same type of research twice, but rather continue to identify new problem areas.

In Latin America there is no significant tradition in applied or action-oriented research centers. To a large extent, the academic concept of research and the lack of demand have kept science away from the problems associated with the development process. Trist[1]

has identified the emergence of this type of research center during
the last 30 years as the most significant characteristic of the evolution of social science research, extrapolating his findings to the
natural and physical sciences.

Research Units in Enterprises and Other Users of Knowledge

Research units in enterprises have as their main function the
solution of immediate problems faced by the users of scientific and
technological knowledge. The research undertaken by these units
is highly utilitarian and has a relatively small content of new knowledge, in comparison with research undertaken by the other types of
units mentioned above. Their main task is to allow productive units
and social agencies to carry out their activities with greater effectiveness.

The programs of these units should be oriented toward improving manufacturing processes, product quality, the use of raw materials, the provision of social services, and so on. Because of the
weaknesses of research and development and the low demand for
local scientific and technological activities, there is a relatively
small number of research units of this type in Latin America, although the situation is beginning to change in countries such as
Brazil, Argentina, Mexico, and Peru. No subsidiary functions are
usually ascribed to these units, and their existence is justified only
in terms of their actual impact on the performance of the organizations to which they are attached.

Units for Popular Participation in Research Tasks

The basic premise behind popular participation units is that
there is a large capacity for the generation and modification of technical knowledge, constituted by the practical knowledge and the experience acquired by the great majority of the labor force, and this
capacity has not been effectively used. The lack of rigor, of conceptual dexterity, and the communication barriers--as well as the
lack of attention paid by scientists and professionals--have not allowed the workers to channel their experience and practical knowledge directly toward systematic problem solving. However, it should
be possible to surmount these difficulties with the support that professionals and scientists can provide, in an organized way, through
units for popular participation in research.

The idea is to organize--in an enterprise, in a group of enterprises, in cooperatives, or in other organizations--ways of channeling individual inventiveness for the improvement of social and productive activities: for example, formal and informal structures that allow the workers to take direct charge of the operations they are performing and be responsible for the modification of the routine that was passed on to them. Development strategies that consider increased popular participation in productive activities and in the management of the economy should explicitly incorporate ways of channeling the inventive capacity of workers at all levels for the generation and modification of technical knowledge. Units for popular participation in research are vehicles through which it may be possible to combine the inventive activity derived from the experience and practical knowledge of the workers with that derived from rigorous training in the scientific method and its systematic application in research.

This type of center is practically unknown in Latin America, with the possible exception of Cuba, and only countries like the People's Republic of China,[2] Norway, and Czechoslovakia have experimented with them. This particular approach has also been suggested in order to combine scientific research and traditional technologies in rural areas.[3]

THE ROLE OF THE UNIVERSITY IN THE GENERATION AND MODIFICATION OF KNOWLEDGE

With the background of the normative conceptial framework that describes the types of research units involved in the generation and modification of knowledge, it is now possible to examine the role that the university should play in the process of building up an autonomous scientific and technological capacity, particularly through the development of an adequate infrastructure for the performance of research activities.

Creating a Local Scientific and Technological Capacity

There are some differences among the Latin American educators, professionals, and scientists who have examined this problem, but in general, all agree that the university can and must play the dominant role in the creation of a local scientific and technological capacity. For example, Darcy Ribeiro[4] considers that the university should adopt an activist stance in the creation and dissemination of technological knowledge, when he speaks of a "diffusing university."

Amilcar Herrera,[5] in his analysis of the social changes taking place in Peru and the consequent changes that the universities must undergo, suggests that the university should take the initiative in changing the structure of science and technology, orienting them toward the concrete problems of development. Oswald Sunkel[6] awards the university the primary role of orienting and performing scientific and technological activities. Edgardo Boeninger endorses the following statement of the Council of University Presidents in Chile:

> . . . the university must, by force, participate more fully in the fields of applied research and experimental development, from the analysis of the fundamental principles of technology, the confirmation of existing theories and new postulates, to the studies of industrial development, passing through laboratory and pilot plant research, design of equipment and reactors, selection of materials, etc. [7]

Although the authors who adopt this point of view do not explicitly reject the use of other institutional forms to develop a scientific and technological capacity, implicitly they ignore institutional structures that are not directly linked to the university. But research, however important it may be, is only a secondary activity for the university, whose central mission is to prepare responsible scientists and professionals to participate actively in the process of development. As José Ortega y Gasset pointed out more than 40 years ago, research has only limited importance in the human development tasks of the university:

> There is no reason whatsoever . . . why the average man (to whom university education should be oriented) need or should be a scientific man. Scandalous consequence: science in its own sense, that is, scientific research, does not belong in an immediate and constitutive manner to the primary functions of the university, neither is it inherently related to them. [8]

Ortega y Gasset refers strictly to science as the creation of new knowledge and considers that its place in a university is subordinated to the teaching function; that is, science in the university is to be pursued primarily because of its contribution to the educational process. This point of view is very far from awarding the university the central role in the development of scientific and technological capabilities.

The experience of other countries outside Latin America shows a variety of institutional arrangements to promote and carry out research and development. In the Eastern European countries, the academies of science and state research institutes have played a dominant role in the creation of scientific and technological knowledge. In Western Europe and the United States this task has been carried out in large measure by private enterprises, independent and government research organizations, and to a lesser extent by universities.

Apart from the fact that historically the majority of scientific and technological research in Latin America has been carried out in universities, there is no justification for giving the university the protagonist's role in the development of an infrastructure for science and technology. Furthermore, considering that university research has been traditionally divorced from the social and economic needs of the Latin American countries, and that the universities are undergoing a series of transformations in which their central mission-- that of forming a new Latin American man--is being questioned, criticized, and reformulated, it cannot be expected that the university will take the leadership and become the dominant institution in the development of a scientific and technological infrastructure.

The importance of building up an indigenous capacity for science and technology in an autonomous development process has already been pointed out. The importance of forming a new Latin American man, professional and scientist, with a culture of his own, with a clear awareness of his condition of underdevelopment, and with a realistic vision of the future, is taken for granted. It is not possible to expect both functions to be properly executed by a single institution, and the second has greater priority as the central mission of the university.

This does not imply that research should be abandoned by universities, or that subordinating research to the educational function would lead to second-rate universities. The instrumental role of research in the educational process has already been underscored. It does imply that the university should not be the leading institution in the development of a scientific and technological capacity, and that it is necessary to develop new institutional forms, with the full support of the university. [9]

Priorities for University Action

Coming back to the types of research units described in the preceding section, it is possible to define priorities for university action in the creation of an infrastructure for science and technology.

In this regard, the university must play a dual role: in some cases it should develop research units within the university, and in others it should promote their establishment outside the university, even if this implies an apparent loss of resources and researchers.

The first priority for university action should be to establish research units for undergraduate education. This is consistent and compatible with the central mission of the university and will help to carry it out more effectively. For this purpose, training in research must become an integral part of the curriculum. Oscar Varsavsky[10] has proposed a way in which this could be done in Peruvian universities. The second priority corresponds to the support that the university should give to the creation and consolidation of applied or action-oriented research units outside the universities. This implies not only giving political support to such units, but also being willing to transfer part of their personnel and resources to them. The main task of applied and action-oriented research units is to produce the knowledge necessary for social and productive activities. The central task of the university is to prepare cadres trained to participate actively in the development process. The organizational structures, internal stability, the relevance of ideological positions, the temporal horizons for action, and many other factors show significant differences for the two sets of institutions that ought to fulfill these two missions. One kind of institution cannot do both of them at the same time.

With a shortsighted vision, to support the creation of research centers outside the university, particularly when this may involve the loss of resources and personnel, may appear to be the wrong strategy for the university. With a long-term perspective this is not the case for several reasons. First, in supporting these research centers the university would be fulfilling one of its secondary functions, that of promoting the development of science and technology in the country. Second, in separating the teaching functions from those of carrying out applied and action-oriented research, the university would be focusing on its central educational mission and would be able to devote more effort and attention to it. Third, in actively promoting the creation of this type of institution the university would be forging interinstitutional links that would allow it to make use of the resources of these centers, through the participation of its researchers as part-time professors, through the use of its equipment and installations, through the demand they may exert for basic research, through the financial support that these research units could give to the university, and through the participation of students in the activities of these research units.[11]

Outside the field of action of universities, the applied or action-oriented research units should count on the maximum possible support from government and the science and technology policy organizations. They are important because of their potential contribution to the development process, particularly in view of the gap that exists between basic research and urgent development needs.

The third priority for university action should be awarded to the creation and reinforcement of graduate educational research units. It is here that the largest share of installed capacity for research in Latin America is found in terms of personnel, equipment, and financial resources. Because of the proliferation of university research centers with dimensions below the necessary minimum critical mass, it is imperative to merge, consolidate, and rationalize the existing set of university research centers.

Finally, the promotion of research units in enterprises and other users of knowledge and promotion of units for popular participation in research are tasks of relatively lesser importance for the university, and they correspond to the organisms in charge of science and technology policy. Nevertheless, the university may be involved in studying the problems associated with the establishment of these units, giving its support to the science and technology policy agencies.

CONCLUSION

One of the necessary conditions for the development of an indigenous capacity for science and technology is to be able to count on an adequate institutional infrastructure to perform all types of scientific and technological activities. The university has an important promotional role in the development of this infrastructure. However, the problem is not one of developing that infrastructure within the university, but rather of seeking a balanced and adequate interinstitutional division of labor. This implies leaving to the universities the research tasks derived directly from educational needs, and promoting the creation and consolidation of institutions outside the university to perform the necessary range of scientific and technological activities. The university need not and should not be the dominant institution in the development of a country's scientific and technological capacity; there are other institutional structures that must be explored and promoted.

NOTES

1. Eric Trist, "Science Policy and the Organization of Research in the Social Sciences," in Main Trends of Research in the Social and Human Sciences (Paris: Mouton/UNESCO, 1970).

2. For the Chinese case see Genevieve Dean, Technology Policies in the People's Republic of China (Ottawa: IDRC, in press).

3. Amilcar Herrera, "Scientific and Traditional Technologies in Developing Countries," Science Policy Research Unit, Sussex University, April 1974. Mimeographed.

4. Darcy Ribeiro, "Política de Desarrollo Autónomo de la Universidad Latinoamericana," in America Latina: Ciencia y Tecnología en el Desarrollo de la Sociedad, ed. Amilcar Herrera (Santiago de Chile: Editorial Universitaria, 1970).

5. Amilcar Herrera, "Bases para Planificar la Investigación Científica en la Universidad Peruana." Report presented to the National Council of Peruvian Universities, Lima, 1972.

6. Oswaldo Sunkel, Reforma Universitaria, Subdesarrollo y Dependencia (Santiago de Chile: Editorial Universitaria, 1969).

7. Edgardo Boeninger, in Hacia una Política de Desarrollo Científico y Tecnológico para Chile (Santiago de Chile: Editorial Universitaria, 1972), p. 28.

8. José Ortega y Gasset, El Libro de las Misiones (Madrid: Espasa-Calpe, 1959), p. 34.

9. One of the few authors who take a similar position to that adopted here is Edmundo Fuenzalida. See his "La Universidad Chilena No Debe Hacer Investigación," in Corporación de Promoción Universitaria, Desarrollo Científico-Tecnológico y Universidad (Santiago de Chile: Ediciones CPU, 1974).

10. Oscar Varsavsky, "Criterios para una Política de Desarrollo Universitario." Report presented to the National Council of Peruvian Universities, Lima, 1972.

11. Marcel Roche in Ch. 10 of his La Ciencia entre Nosotros (Caracas: Ediciones IVIC, 1968) puts forward some ideas on this theme and describes his experience in linking an independent research institution with the universities.

9

Technological Self-Reliance and Cooperation among Third World Countries

SELF-RELIANCE, DEVELOPMENT, AND TECHNOLOGY

During the past ten years the concept of self-reliance has gained importance in the conceptualization of development processes. There have been many proposals suggesting how this concept can be incorporated into development strategies, although there is no clear agreement on its precise content. The intellectual and political roots of the idea of self-reliance span more than a century and have emerged in a variety of situations (witness utopian thinking about autonomous communities), thus making it difficult to identify a meaning for self-reliance that corresponds to a theory of development and applies generally.

The Concept of Self-Reliance

In a review of the current concept of self-reliance Onelia Cardettini[1] traces its origins to Mao's thinking and Gandhian philosophy, pointing out that it has spread—either as a political-philosophical statement or as a component of development strategies—to countries as varied as Algeria, Peru, India, Cuba, Tanzania, China, and the Ivory Coast. The origin of the concern may have been the realization that development aid was grossly insufficient, the will to explore a third road (neither Communist nor capitalist) to development, or the strains imposed by economic and political blockades. Cardettini finds that self-reliance is a deceitfully

———————

Used with permission from a paper first published in <u>World Development</u> 4 (October/November 1976): 939–46.

simple word to define and shows the shortcomings of accepted definitions such as "to rely upon one's own strength" or "to count upon one's own efforts," particularly when they are taken as policy directives. Therefore, in order to integrate the concept of self-reliance into a development strategy, it is necessary to give operational content to the policy directives it implies in a specific area of concern such as financing, food production, and science and technology. Self-reliance in science and technology can be interpreted in three different senses:

As the capacity for autonomous decision making in matters of technology. This has been the approach suggested by several Latin American writers who consider this decision autonomy as a prerequisite to the development of a scientific and technological capacity.[2] In this case it is not necessary to possess the technology to meet development needs within a country. Decision autonomy refers to the capacity for defining technology requirements, identifying alternatives available elsewhere (breaking them into their components), and determining the best way to acquire, incorporate, and absorb the technology. This in turn is related to the capacity for obtaining and processing information about technology.

As the combination of decision autonomy and the capacity to generate independently the critical elements of technical knowledge required for a particular product or process. Products and processes are composed of many elements of technical knowledge, some of which may be critical because they are essential or because of the difficulties in obtaining access to them (for example, a catalyzer in a chemical process, a design in electronic equipment). This capacity is closely linked to the development of engineering design skills and does not necessarily imply that the totality of the critical element is to be produced within a country. What is required is the capability to design the process or product (and its critical elements in particular), to define standards and specifications for the components to be manufactured, and to assemble the components into the complete design.

As the autonomous potential for producing within a country the goods and services considered essential in the development strategy. In this sense technological self-reliance involves autonomy of decision and the possession of technical knowledge and skills, as well as the capacity for transforming them into goods and services. A country is able to rely on its own capabilities if forced to do so, although under normal conditions it does not attempt to engage in all of the productive activities it is capable of performing.

The first interpretation of the concept of self-reliance can be extended to a large variety of areas. It is possible to have an autonomous decision capacity with regard to the means of producing a particular good even when the actual capabilities to produce it are not within reach. This requires having a cadre of professionals and technicians, knowledgeable in each area of concern, as well as access to the information that must be processed to arrive at a decision. The same can be applied to the second interpretation, although the degree of knowledge and skills required will be much greater and directly linked to engineering design capabilities. The third interpretation of the concept of self-reliance encompasses the first two and can be achieved only in selected fields that should be linked to the development strategy. In this case, not only must the cadres and information be available, but also the actual means of production (engineering and managerial capabilities, manufacturing facilities, raw materials, and so on) that enable a country to do without external sources of supply.

Although primarily referring to technology, these interpretations of self-reliance have backward linkages to science. The conduct of scientific activities is necessary to maintain an autonomous decision capacity in the majority of technological fields, particularly in those developing at a rapid pace. Without a base of active scientists and professionals it is almost impossible to follow the evolution of technology and to have a clear perception of available alternatives and options. This is even more true when the technology refers to the performance of activities specific to the country, and for which no suitable alternatives have been developed elsewhere.

However, it is clear that the concept of self-reliance does not apply to the conduct of scientific inquiry as such. Science, considered as a process for generating knowledge, is an international activity, and, in this sense no country can be self-reliant in science. The reasonable approach is to consider the development of scientific capabilities that provide a basis for technological self-reliance.

The Context of Self-Reliance

Dealing with technological self-reliance should not lead one to lose the wider perspective that places it in context. Strong political commitments and internal socioeconomic transformations are necessary for a less developed country to pursue a policy of self-reliance in technology or in any other area. A prerequisite to self-reliance is the attainment of a significant degree of self-control or national independence, meaning by this the freedom to set national objectives and to choose the means of achieving them. This implies a political act of affirmation and the possibility of sustaining it, by neutralizing external and internal interferences, during the time necessary to consolidate the transformations and to set the foundations for the socioeconomic structure envisaged. This act of affirmation should include measures to control investment flows, to modify patterns of consumption, to direct the location of social and productive activities, and to manage the use of natural resources.[3]

These measures will strongly condition the possibility of pursuing a policy of self-reliance in matters of science and technology. The patterns of investment, consumption, location, and resource use determine the nature of the demand for scientific and technological activities. Therefore, it is not possible to be technologically self-reliant while setting widely different policies for other areas of the development strategy. All of these factors must be combined into a coherent style of development and a strategy associated with it, which will determine the extent to which a policy of self-reliance in technology makes sense.[4]

CHANGES IN THE INTERNATIONAL ORDER AND THEIR IMPLICATIONS FOR TECHNOLOGICAL SELF-RELIANCE

The emergence of underdevelopment as a historical phenomenon has been characterized by Celso Furtado in the following terms:

As a consequence of the rapid spread of new production methods from a small number of centres radiating technological innovations, there has come into existence a process tending to create a world-wide economic system. It is thus that underdevelopment is considered a creature of development, or rather, as a consequence of the impact of the technical processes and the international division of labour commanded by the small number of societies that espoused the Industrial Revolution in the nineteenth century. The resulting relations between these societies and the underdeveloped areas involve forms of dependence that can hardly be overcome. The dependence was initially based on an international division of labour in which the dominant centres reserved for themselves the economic activities that concentrated technical progress. In the following phase, the dependence was maintained by controlling the assimilation of new technological processes through the installation

of productive activities within the dependent economies,
all under the control of groups integrated into the
dominant economies.[5]

Change in Dominant Relations

There is evidence that the nature of the process described by
Furtado regarding the relations between dominant and dominated
economies is continuing and changing at a rapid pace. The next
phase in this process consists in a shift toward the control of financial resources,[6] and a transition toward the use of technological
knowledge as the main vehicle for maintaining the relations of domination is now evident. Thus there has been a gradual (although in-
complete) displacement of the means of control of developed countries over underdeveloped ones from raw materials, to productive
facilities, to capital and finance, and now to technology. In this
process of mutation of dominant relations, technology has always
been in the background as a conditioning factor, but it has now
finally emerged into the open, partly because of the internal dynamics of the evolution of the capitalist economic system, and
partly because of the increased control of the less developed countries over the means through which the developed countries exerted
their domination in the past.

Two excerpts from statements by leaders of Western industrialized countries may show the extent to which this transformation
of dominant relationships is taking place. U.S. Secretary of State
Henry Kissinger, in an address to the General Assembly of the
Organization of American States (April 20, 1974), said that:

> The transfer of science and technology may be an even
> more important bottleneck in the development effort than
> capital. The United States, as a technologically ad-
> vanced nation, recognizes a special responsibility in
> this regard. We believe that normally private invest-
> ment is the most efficient vehicle for the large-scale
> transfer of these resources, but governments can
> facilitate the transfer of advanced technology to stimu-
> late balanced development. [Emphasis added.]

In a speech delivered at a session of the European Parliament in
early 1975, Xanier Ortoli, president of the Commission of European
Communities, stated:

> While continuing the financial aid which is indispensable
> for certain countries, we must wherever possible work
> for cooperation based on long-term economic links,
> which are a better instrument of progress and solidarity
> than any treaty. While respecting our partner's own
> objectives, we should combine our technology and know-
> how, our markets, in certain cases our capital and our
> products, in particular agricultural, with our partners'
> resources and their desire to take advantage of the new
> situation for their development. [Emphasis added.]

Recent statements made by Henry Kissinger at the UNCTAD IV meeting in Nairobi confirm the interest of Western leaders in the technology issue, and it is clear that it will acquire greater prominence in the years to come, particularly as the Third World countries increase their control over their own natural resources. There will be a trend to use the access to technology as the main lever in North-South dominating relations, with the subsidiary use of food, and in some cases capital, to complement it.[7]

Under these circumstances the importance of technological self-reliance cannot be underestimated. There is an urgent need to take the measures that will provide the Third World countries with a minimum of means to confront this new situation. In fact, the possibility of following an independent road to development will be determined by the extent to which a country is technologically self-reliant. This requires the establishment of an overall strategy for technological self-reliance, defining the areas in which each of the different interpretations of the concept is to be applied, their inter-relations, and the time in which they can be achieved.

Development Style and Strategy

It has been pointed out earlier that technological self-reliance cannot be pursued out of the context of an autonomous development style and strategy. Therefore, the issues of technological self-reliance and alternative development styles interact with each other, to the extent that they cannot be considered independently. Technological self-reliance is incompatible with a style of development that maintains the present mode of dependent insertion of the underdeveloped countries into the world economic system. It can be realized fully only within the context of a development style and strategy that modify significantly a country's international position. However, effecting the changes that will allow the less developed countries to follow their own paths to development requires concerted action, for most of them do not have the power to bring about the necessary changes in the international situation on their own: collective efforts are required to pursue independent development strategies.

There is an apparent contradiction in the need to collaborate with others in the search for self-reliance, although this apparent contradiction disappears when collaboration is viewed as a process of joining forces by countries with the same basic interests, that is, the underdeveloped countries. In principle any form of alliance implies certain limitations on individual freedom, but these limitations need not interfere with the main orientation chosen for a country's development process.

Summarizing, the attainment of self-reliance in matters of technology requires that an independent development strategy be followed. Also, technological self-reliance conditions the possibility of pursuing an independent development strategy. Both imply the need for breaking a country's dependent mode of insertion into the world economy and seeking new ways of linking up with it. Finally, significant changes in the forms of insertion of underdeveloped countries can be achieved only through concerted action by those who stand to gain from these changes. This provides a powerful argument for promoting cooperation among underdeveloped countries, particularly when related to the pursuit of technological self-reliance.

DISTRIBUTION OF SCIENTIFIC AND TECHNOLOGICAL EFFORT AND ITS IMPACT ON SELF-RELIANCE

In the second half of the twentieth century it is possible to observe a process of concentration in the sources of technological change, which is imposed at the world level—and at an ever-increasing pace—by a relatively small number of advanced countries and large enterprises. The characteristics of this process are the high degree of interdependence between military interests and industrial concerns, to which the space industry was added in the 1960s, which biases the nature of technological progress; and the increased interconnection among the research and development interests of large multinational enterprises, one of the central facets of what has been called the Global Industrial System. Both of these characteristics show that the rate and direction of technical change at present are determined to a very large extent by interests that have nothing to do with the aspirations and goals of underdeveloped countries. Furthermore, the degree of concentration is getting so high that a limited number of executives from large corporations and government officials in developed countries can exert a decisive influence on the nature of technical change at the world level.

At the same time this process of concentration is going on, the minimum critical mass to engage in viable scientific and technological efforts is increasing. On the basis of an analysis of a minimum number of research institutes of various types, Herrera[8] concluded that in 1970 at least U.S. $100 million were required to sustain a viable scientific and technological system. He did not include the costs of transforming research results into products or processes, and since his calculations were made, the cost of scientific and technological activities has undoubtedly increased. Other estimates put the threshold of expenditures for a viable scientific and technological system at 1 percent of the GNP. These figures provide only a general idea about minimum requirements, but they give an indication that few underdeveloped countries now have capacity to engage in the construction of an independently viable scientific and technological system. When figures on qualified manpower are examined, they lead to a similar conclusion.

Furthermore, because of the small size of the internal market of most underdeveloped countries, there are also limitations to the bargaining power they can exert when entering into deals with suppliers of technology from developed countries. In addition, the high cost and the difficulties in obtaining access to information sources, which would improve bargaining positions, make it practically impossible for most underdeveloped countries to acquire the relevant information on their own.

The need to alter the world-wide distribution of resources for science and technology and to break the high degree of concentration in the sources of technological change, the need to exceed the minimum critical mass in order to have viable scientific and technological systems, and the need to improve bargaining position in the acquisition of technology, lead to the imperative of cooperation in science and technology matters among underdeveloped countries. It will be impossible to follow a policy of technological self-reliance unless this condition is met, for the obstacles a country will encounter are too great to be overcome individually.

However, experience has shown that cooperation agreements are relatively easier to reach when issues of a purely scientific nature are involved, but that when cooperation programs involve scientific and technological activities that may have direct economic application, agreement is more difficult to obtain. Thus, effective joint programs will require a new spirit of collaboration among Third World countries, on the basis of which relative short-term gains for a particular country should be viewed as temporary imbalances along the road to collective efforts toward technological self-reliance.

Only after a certain degree of cohesion among the underdeveloped countries has been achieved through concrete collaborative arrangements will it be possible to engage in the process of restructuring the insertion of a particular country into the world scientific and technological system. In effect this implies a two-step strategy in which increased Third World cooperation is seen as a prerequisite to new forms of collaboration between underdeveloped and developed countries.

POSSIBLE CONTENT OF COOPERATION AGREEMENTS

Once the imperative of Third World cooperation for the achievement of technological self-reliance is accepted, the task is to identify suitable areas for collaboration, to obtain political commitments, and to design specific programs. Among the possible areas where such programs may be instituted are:

Activities that require a minimum critical mass to be performed. This includes research and development for which it is necessary to depend on professionals, equipment, and financing at a level below which the activities are not viable. In these fields it is impossible to intervene individually and cooperation efforts are indispensable.

Scientific and technological activities in which there are economies of scale (information systems, training programs, engineering capabilities, common research and development, and so on). In this case international cooperation is not absolutely necessary, but involves many benefits that make it highly desirable.

Activities that must involve an international dimension to make sense. This includes comparative and joint actions that are meaningless when considered in only one country. An example is the establishment of comparative information systems on terms and conditions for technology transfer, which would increase the bargaining power of the countries buying technology. This can be extended to agreeing on common strategies for negotiations with technology suppliers and to the adoption of common positions before multinational corporations, multilateral financial institutions, and other similar organizations.

Problems common to more than one country, linked to geographical zones that extend beyond national frontiers. This includes research into ecological conditions, the exploitation of natural resources, use of water systems, and so on. In this case the existence of a common problem provides countries with the possibility of joining forces in the performance of scientific and technological activities.

Large undertakings in which it is necessary to share risks among several countries because of the magnitude of resources required. This has been the case of investments in nuclear energy, computers, satellite telecommunications, and so on, in which few individual countries—even if they are capable of financing the program on their own—are willing to take the risk alone.

If technological cooperation takes place within a context of wider political and economic integration, additional fields for international collaboration among less developed countries emerge.[9] Among these are the common exploitation of certain technologies which, because of scale, are viable only in terms of an expanded market. The harmonization of national economic policies for the pursuit of self-reliance can also be included here, as well as the search for technologies for joint economic development projects. The full benefits of increased cooperation for technological self-reliance can be realized only when they are considered an integral part of a broader process of economic and political cooperation.

Establishing a system of cooperation in science and technology matters may require a reformulation of concepts, such as "region," that have traditionally been used to define groups among the underdeveloped countries. Problem-centered regions can be defined in terms of the need to embark on joint programs for the solution of specific technological problems. Thus a region for scientific and technological cooperation in the Third World may comprise countries that are geographically scattered, that do not share the same cultural heritage, and that have different political systems. The common characteristics grouping them are the problem area and the will to engage jointly in activities that will help in its solution.

Another area for Third World cooperation arises out of the need to confront the process of rapid technological change that is at present a feature of the evolution of the world economy. Underdeveloped countries receive the impact of technological changes without understanding their nature, appreciating their implications, and even without realizing that the directions taken by their own development are conditioned to a large extent by the nature and the sources of technological change. Although it is feasible to examine the social impacts of technological changes, the underdeveloped countries have seldom examined them in detail. New industries are located in rural zones without an adequate understanding of the social and cultural effects, communications and transport methods are adopted without assessing their indirect effects, interregional transport and urban development are promoted without taking into account the dynamics of rural-urban interactions, new agricultural techniques are adopted without due examination of their relation to

existing cultural and social patterns, tourism is promoted without
an understanding of the processes of value transfer that it implies,
and so on. This list could be expanded almost indefinitely, and
points out that the achievement of self-reliance requires the development of a capacity to assess the impact of technological change.
The development of this capacity will probably exceed the limits of
individual action and thus provides another reason for increased
cooperation among underdeveloped countries.

However, there are also many obstacles to the organization
of viable cooperation programs among underdeveloped countries.
The heterogeneity of political regimes and orientations has often
proved to be a major difficulty, even when cooperation refers to
scientific matters. Also the different levels of development, particularly with regard to science and technology, make it difficult
to organize cooperation programs in which all the participants can
improve their knowledge and level of skills to the same degree.
These two factors generate frictions that may impede the launching
and consolidation of cooperation agreements. Furthermore, many
Third World countries are subjected to pressures from industrialized countries, international organizations and financing agencies,
and foreign experts from advanced countries, all of which stand to
lose some influence if collaborative programs among underdeveloped
countries expand significantly. Finally, there are also obstacles
that arise out of the behavior of the scientific and engineering communities in Third World countries, such as the distrust of institutions and researchers from other underdeveloped countries (preference for linking up with the advanced centers of learning), and the
fact that many group privileges are associated with travel and extended stays in the industrialized countries; these, in turn, may be
a reflection of the insufficient decolonization of the mind.

Therefore, any strategy to expand cooperation among underdeveloped countries for the purpose of achieving technological
self-reliance must be gradual and flexible, exploiting every possible opportunity, but taking into account the obstacles that may
thwart the first efforts. The establishment of a scientific and
technical tradition in any country is a lengthy process, which becomes even more lengthy and difficult when the dimension of international cooperation is added to it.

A POSSIBLE FRAMEWORK FOR ORGANIZING
THIRD WORLD COOPERATION FOR
TECHNOLOGICAL SELF-RELIANCE

There are many ways of organizing cooperation in science and
technology among developing countries.[10] The choice and design of

a particular framework will depend on the nature of the problem to be tackled, the perception of common interests by the concerned parties, their degree of political commitment, and the level of capabilities that can be marshaled. Considering the number of participant countries and the structure of their relations, the modes of cooperation may be classified into specific bilateral, broad bilateral, specific multilateral, broad multilateral, regional, and community. Each of these modes has particular advantages and disadvantages, and hence there is no universal best solution for organizing cooperation efforts.*

Bilateral programs respond to the interests of two particular countries and there is relatively little that can be said about their structure or convenience as a general model. Regional and community cooperation depend on the existence of broader frameworks of regional or community economic cooperation, for which it is necessary to have political commitments of wider scope. Hence, only multilateral programs will be discussed here.

The existing structure of multilateral international organizations, most of which include both developed and underdeveloped countries, performs useful functions in a variety of fields. However, there is a need to complement their activities with new forms of organization that have greater flexibility, operate at lesser cost, and respond more directly and rapidly to the need for cooperation among underdeveloped countries for the attainment of technological self-reliance. One possibility is to structure a dual framework consisting of a general agreement for broad multilateral cooperation, together with a variety of specific multilateral agreements.

The idea is to establish an international association with a large membership of underdeveloped countries from all regions in the world.† Membership would entail sharing in the support of a

---

*The United Nations Development Program (UNDP) organized a series of regional conferences during 1976 and 1977 on the topic of Technical Cooperation among Developing Countries (TCDC), in which the various mechanisms for international cooperation were examined. A U.N. general conference on the subject took place in 1978 in Buenos Aires.

†The group of nonaligned countries would constitute a natural basis for the organization of this association and at the August 1975 Meeting of Ministers of Foreign Affairs in Lima, the establishment of a cooperation scheme similar to the one suggested here was approved. It was further discussed at an experts' meeting in New York and approved at the Conference of Heads of State in Sri Lanka in August 1976.

small central staff, whose main task would be to identify, structure, and launch science and technology projects to be undertaken by member countries. The projects could involve research, technology adaption, negotiation with technology suppliers, training, and other activities linked to the pursuit of technological self-reliance. Not every country would participate in each project, although it would be expected that every country would participate in at least one project during a reasonable time period. The association could be established through a broad multilateral agreement signed by all member countries, and the projects would be launched through specific multilateral agreements among the countries interested in them.

The central staff would consult with the relevant institutions in the member countries in order to determine priorities for the identification and design of research projects. It is envisaged that a small group of highly qualified professionals, nominated for a fixed term (for example, five years), would form the central staff. They would be assisted by consultants working for short periods. The central staff itself would not be directly engaged in research as their main activity, although they could participate actively in some specific research projects. Financing for the central staff would be assured by member-country contributions, and possibly by funds from international organizations and donor agencies. Thus it would not be a significant drain on the member countries' foreign exchange resources. It is clear that the central staff would be located in a Third World country. A supervisory board elected by the member countries would oversee the functions of the central staff.

Specific projects would be carried out in selected institutions of the participating countries in a decentralized way. The projects would be temporary and would have a coordinating committee—which would direct the conduct of each project—consisting of one representative from each participating country. If found necessary, there could also be an executive project coordinator accountable to the committee. In this way no permanent organizational structure would be created around the projects. At a given moment in time there would be several specific projects under way, others in the gestation period, and still others that had been completed. The organizational arrangements will depend on the nature and scope of the problems to be tackled, for some may require the existence of a central laboratory and others may be handled in a completely decentralized way. Flexibility should be maintained in this respect.

The framework outlined for Third World cooperation in the pursuit of technological self-reliance would lead to a process of identifying common interests, organizing specific cooperation activities, and applying the results in accordance with the interests and the objectives of a given particular country. It would generate a process of forging, severing, and restructuring links in accordance with changing needs and capabilities for the purpose of achieving self-reliance in matters of technology. Unless concrete actions are taken in the short term by the underdeveloped countries—organizing a cooperation framework like the one proposed here, or putting into effect any other form of collaborative arrangements—self-reliance in technology will remain an illusion for most of the Third World.

NOTES

1. Oneila Cardettini, "Technological Dependence/Self-reliance: An Introductory Statement," STPI Project, Office of the Field Coordinator, Lima, May 1976.

2. See, for example, Jorge Sabato, Ciencia, Tecnología, Dependencia (Tucuman, Argentina: Ed. Mensaje, 1971).

3. These concepts are developed for the case of Peru in J. Bravo Bresani, Francisco Sagasti, and Augusto Salazar Bondy, El Reto del Perú en la Perspectiva del Tercer Mundo (Lima: Moncloa Editors, 1972).

4. For interpretations of self-reliance in a wider context see The Cocoyoc Declaration, United Nations Environment Program (UNEP)/UNCTAD, October 1974; What to Do, report of the Dag Hammarskjold Foundation, Uppsala, June 1975; and Wilbert K. Chagula, Bernard T. Feld, and Ashok Parthasarati, eds., Pugwash on Self-Reliance (New Delhi: Ankur Publishing House, 1977).

5. Celso Furtado, Obstacles to Development in Latin America (New York: Anchor Books, 1970), p. xvi.

6. See Maria C. Tavares, Da Substituiçao de Importaçoes ao Capitalismo Financiero (Rio de Janeiro: Zahar Editores, 1972); and Ricardo Tolipan, "Tecnologá e Produçao Capitalista," Cuadernos CEBRAP (Centro Brasileiro de Planejamiento e Analise), no. 13, pp. 37-59.

7. On these issues, see Máximo Halty, "Towards a New Technological Order?" Paper presented at the OECD seminar on Science, Technology and Development in a Changing World, Paris, April 1975.

8. Amilcar Herrera, Ciencia y Política en América Latina (Mexico: Siglo XXI, 1971).

9. See Francisco Sagasti, "Integración Económica y Política Tecnológica, el Caso del Pacto Andino," Comercio Exterior 25 no. 1 (January 1975): 46-49, and in Revista de la Integración, no. 18 (January-March 1975), pp. 169-81.

10. These issues are examined in further detail in Francisco Sagasti and Mauricio Guerrero, El Desarrollo Científico y Tecnológico de América Latina (Buenos Aires: BID/INTAL, 1974).

10

*Reflections on the Endogenization
of the Scientific-Technological
Revolution
in Underdeveloped Countries*

INTRODUCTION

Throughout the history of mankind, and particularly during the
last five centuries, it has been possible to observe an evolution in
the way in which natural and social phenomena have been assessed.
The prevailing perspective from which men have examined and ex-
plained the world they live in has moved from magic to religion and
then to science, although this evolution has not been linear and complete, and it is still possible to find magic and religion coexisting
and competing with the scientific perspective.[1] In this process of
evolution of thought the main contribution from the West has been the
use of reason, and specifically the scientific method deriving from
it, to contrast mental schemes with the evidence of the senses, thus
building a cumulative fabric of knowledge whose weft is abstract concepts and whose warp is empiric observations.

The pursuit of science, considered as an organized, continuous,
and self-correcting process of knowledge generation, plays at present
a most significant role in the progress of productive and social activities, to such an extent that it can be considered the main driving force
for growth, particularly in the developed countries. This is an age
that can be characterized by the predominance of technology that is
in some way or other related to scientific findings.

In international relations this is reflected in the fact that a few
developed countries currently control the generation of, and access
to, modern technology. Furthermore, these countries count on a
surplus of food and capital which they interchange with the underde-

Used with permission from a paper published in <u>Science and
Public Policy</u> 4 (December 1977): 504-13.

veloped countries for natural resources and energy. Under excep-
tional circumstances the latter may have sufficient food or capital,
but as has been demonstrated in several instances (recently after
the price increase of oil in 1973-74, which produced a massive transfer of financial resources to the OPEC member countries, but clearly
highlighted their technological dependence), the developed countries
are the only ones capable of fully linking a self-sustaining base of
scientific activities with production. As a consequence, they control
the access to modern technology and are thus capable of tilting the
balance in their favor (see Chapter 9).[2]

It should also be noted that food surpluses in these countries
are a result of the application of technologies based on or related to
scientific findings (fertilizers, pesticides, mechanical equipment),
and that their capital surplus arises from the use of high-productivity
techniques that lead to a process of accumulation that goes well beyond the needs of capital replacement. In this way, science-related
technologies have been and are at the root of an international order
that classifies nations as developed or underdeveloped.

For the purpose of this study, two types of countries will be
distinguished: those in which the evolution of scientific activity has
led directly to, or has clearly been linked with, advances in production techniques; and those in which the knowledge-generating activity
has not been related in any significant way to productive activities.
The first will be referred to as countries with an endogenous scientific and technological base, and the second as countries with an
exogenous scientific and technological base, noting that this distinction corresponds to that made between developed and underdeveloped
countries.

COUNTRIES WITH AN ENDOGENOUS
SCIENTIFIC-TECHNOLOGICAL BASE

Whether as the result of an internal cumulative process (as in
Western Europe), or of a transplant that later on grew its own roots
(as in the United States and Japan), in these parts of the world the
systematic generation of knowledge and the production of goods and
services are linked organically through the development of techniques
related to scientific findings. New knowledge is transformed into
products without the need of resorting to substantial external assistance, except for the normal process of contrasting scientific findings.
The emergence of scientific and technological capabilities in the West
can be understood by examining the evolution of ideas that led to
science, the successive transformations of productive techniques,
and the merging of these two currents.

Evolution of Western Thought and Productive Activities

In considering briefly the evolution of Western thought, it is necessary to go back as far as the Hellenic period. From the pre-Socratic philosophers, who began to elaborate abstractions of the world surrounding them--to Plato, who contributed to the conceptualization of ideals--and to Aristotle, who formalized logic and the concept of method, the ability to build and relate concepts abstracted from reality was first developed in Greece. During the period of the Roman Empire and the Middle Ages no new elements were added to the Greek conceptual structure, and this was to a large extent related to the prevailing view of a certain divine order imposed on mankind and to the predominance of dogmatic disquisitions. However, the influence of the Arab world on Europe toward the end of the Middle Ages helped in the development of schemes for manipulating concepts and symbols (for example, algebra), and motivated a return to the examination of natural phenomena (witness the concerns of the alchemists).[3]

The Renaissance brought a revaluation of manual labor and of detailed observation, which was to facilitate the full contrast between abstract concepts and physical phenomena, thus paving the road for modern science. Philosophers began to worry about machines, systematic astronomical observations helped navigation, and the renewed respect for manual labor (which had been looked down upon during the Middle Ages) reached its culmination with the work of great artists such as da Vinci. The contributions of Copernicus and Galileo on the celestial order led to the triumph of reason over dogma, and constituted a milestone in the transition from religion to science as a way of explaining natural phenomena. Finally, the contribution of Newton, who introduced the idea that the universe was predictable and obeyed certain laws that could be known and tested, radically changed man's conception of the world, giving sense to the Baconian statement that man can master and control nature through understanding.

Considering now the techniques used in productive activities, the Middle Ages and the Renaissance saw a cumulative evolution of the crafts practiced by artisans, which were gradually transformed into manufacturing activities, and later, during the seventeenth century, into true industrial activities. The achievement that marked this transition was the use of machines to manufacture machines, referred to by Marx as the "emergence of large-scale industry."[4] This took place concurrently with a gradual but relentless shift from a polytechnic era of varied local technological responses, usually in harmony with the environment (although there were exceptions such as the environmental contamination in London due to coal utilization during the thirteenth and 14th centuries), toward a monotechnic era in which the variety of responses is reduced and a few specific production technologies predominate in each field of activity.[5]

Science and Production

The merger of both currents--the evolution of thinking and the evolution of technology--constituted what has been referred to as the scientific and technological revolution. This was a complex process, full of sinuosities and blind alleys, where science on the one hand and productive techniques on the other interacted strongly and conditioned each other. This process lasted approximately 200 years, starting in the mid-seventeenth century, and has provoked heated debates on the relative contribution of the two currents.[6] Broadly speaking, it appears that during an early stage craftsmen and manufacturers made a greater contribution to the growth of science (especially to its experimental aspects through the construction of instruments) than that made by scientists to the productive activities of artisans and industrialists. However, toward the end of the period, the findings related to mechanics, chemistry, optics, thermodynamics, and other areas of knowledge were making a perhaps larger contribution to the development of production techniques, than were the latter to the development of science. The point of inflection marking the beginning of the predominance of science-related technologies over the techniques that evolved in a gradual and autonomous way was the emergence of the first productive activities based on scientific findings: the electric and chemical industries. Since then, the contributions of science to production have been growing at an accelerated pace.

This merger took place among considerable social upheavals, concurrently with the emergence of capitalism as the dominant system, and with the spread of the market economy at the European and international levels.[7] There is no need to reproduce here the debate on whether progress in science and technology was a key contributing factor in the rise of capitalism, or whether capitalism led to the rapid growth of scientific and technological activities. The important issue is that both phenomena were closely intertwined and were exclusive to the development of the West.

The marriage of science and production, as well as the concurrent social upheavals, took place while techniques of lower relative efficiency were being abandoned, in accordance with the economic criteria prevailing at the time. The process of reduction in the variety of technological responses, which started toward the end of the Middle Ages, was suddenly accelerated to such an extent that in many cases it totally disrupted the cumulative development of traditional technologies, and led to what Mumford called "the loss of the polytechnic heritage."[8]

The subsequent evolution of the interactions among science, technology, and production in the countries with an endogenous scientific-technological base is well known. The accelerated pace of technological progress during the last hundred years has been extensively documented and only a few milestones will be pointed out here--such as the replacement of the individual researcher by organized laboratories (referred to by Sabato as the emergence of technology factories),[9] which started about 1890 and is now widespread; the incipient use of warfare technologies based on scientific findings during World War I (for example, mustard gas); and the diffusion of technological knowledge and values brought about by the improvement of the internal combustion engine and the massive production of automobiles. The period between the two world wars witnessed great advances in physics, which culminated with the development of the atomic bomb, and in chemistry, which led to the widespread production of new synthetic materials. Finally, the World War II and postwar periods may be characterized as the age of the scientific explosion, in which the advances in electronics, biology, chemistry, cybernetics, and many other fields transformed science into the key source of changes and improvements in production techniques. In countries with an endogenous scientific-technological base, this was associated with an increase in the minimum critical mass of resources required to develop science and by an unprecedented expansion in the scientific-technological effort, to such an extent that Fritz Machlup could state that in 1960 more than one-third of the economically active population of the United States was linked in one way or other to the "knowledge industry" (research, teaching, information, and so on).[10]

Retrospectively, in those countries with an endogenous scientific-technological base the last 400 years have witnessed the emergence of the profession of generating knowledge in an organized and cumulative way, and have seen the evolution from science practiced by individuals to that carried out by an incipient collectivity of scientists, and to that currently undertaken by a full-fledged scientific community. This community acquired legitimacy not only because of the increasingly coherent explanations it gave to natural and, to a lesser extent, social phenomena, but mainly because it demonstrated its usefulness for the development of production techniques, a usefulness anticipated by Bacon in the early seventeenth century when he stated that knowledge in itself is the source of power. It is appropriate to add that the scientific community has

not remained static. Joseph Ben-David[11] has pointed out the shift
of the center of gravity of scientific activity from Italy to the Nether-
lands, England, France, Germany, and later to the United States,
over a period of four centuries and without loss of continuity.

Perhaps the most important feature of the scientific-technological revolution, referred to by Simon Kuznets as an "epoch-
making innovation,"[12] was the discovery and improvement of the
methodology of invention, which, building on the foundations initially
laid by the Greeks, allowed the limitations of the materials and procedures resulting from the slow and gradual process of technological
evolution to be transcended. Once this barrier was crossed, the
possibilities opened up were enormous--bounded primarily by the
possible advances in the amount of knowledge and the limitations of
the human mind.

However, the illusion that this was a conscious, orderly, and
planned undertaking must be dispelled. Rather, it took place in a
spontaneous fashion, covering a wide spectrum of areas, with duplication of efforts, many false starts, and a series of contradictions.
Nevertheless, the self-corrective nature of science allowed for
changes in course to be effected, although always within the broad
directions determined by the conjunction of the interests of scientists and those of states and institutions financing scientific activities. Incidentally, it is in response to these interests that at present more than half of the world resources channeled to science and
technology are devoted to the improvement of warfare technologies.

Another feature associated with the symbiosis of scientific and
productive activities has been the diffusion through society of the
values and modes of thinking related to the scientific-technological
revolution. The idea that it is possible to understand, predict, and
control observed phenomena, that men are able to overcome the
limitations imposed by nature, has influenced greatly the development of countries with an endogenous scientific and technological
base, in contrast to those in which traditional concepts and values,
linked to magical or religious perspectives, have hampered the full
utilization of man's faculties and potentialities.

COUNTRIES WITH AN EXOGENOUS
SCIENTIFIC-TECHNOLOGICAL BASE

The majority of the underdeveloped countries, in contrast with
Western European nations and others such as the United States and
Japan, have not established a basis of productive technologies related to scientific findings of their own. There has been no linkage
between the development of activities devoted to the generation of

knowledge and the evolution of production techniques, and with these two areas have remained completely isolated from each other.

The Nature of Productive Activities

The diffusion of Western science to countries with an exogenous scientific-technological base has been an irregular process, entailing a partial acceptance of results, but without full awareness of the cumulative processes that originated them. The conduct of science in these countries, even to a greater extent than in countries with an endogenous scientific-technological base, has been an activity limited to the elites and isolated pioneers who lacked organic links with their social environment, at least in regard to their scientific-technological activity. Their efforts were inherently out of phase in time, since the frontiers of knowledge were being explored in other parts of the world and they received information on advances and findings with unavoidable delays.

Thus, the pursuit of science did not grow roots in the majority of these countries until the first decades of the twentieth century, and even then it acquired a fragmentary, reflex, and imitative character, divorced from the productive sphere. In some cases, such as India in the nineteenth century, the colonial power deliberately excluded the potential local scientists from research undertaken by the colonizers, thus preventing the development of indigenous scientific-technological capabilities.[13] Science was mainly oriented toward the knowledge-generating world centers, and the concern for local scientific activities arose only insofar as it was necessary to know the environment better for a more intensive exploitation of resources, or insofar as curiosity and the possibility of contributing to the advancement of world knowledge motivated scientists to focus their efforts on specific regional problems.

The nature of productive activities was conditioned first by the interests of the colonial powers and then, after some regions became independent (particularly Latin America), by the way in which their economies were incorporated into the international division of labor accompanying the expansion of the capitalist system. Due to this, productive activities in these countries were oriented primarily toward the extraction of natural resources of interest to the colonizers or capitalists, or to the generation of surplus to be transferred abroad.

Most of the techniques used in productive activities were imported, and this meant that the associated technological base was alien to the local environment. When the implanted extractive and manufacturing activities began to acquire greater relative importance in the local economy, the corresponding technological capabilities were expanded through new technology imports. As a result, these countries acquired a reflex and superficial layer of technical knowledge, disconnected from their physical and social realities, which depended on additional knowledge from abroad for its maintenance and renovation.

The Traditional Technological Base

Considering now the traditional technological base, it is possible to say that after a relatively short lapse at the beginning of the colonial period, during which colonizers learned to operate in an alien environment, the indigenous non-Western technological tradition, which had been developing slowly and cumulatively for a long time (through a process similar to that which took place in Europe during the Middle Ages), was eliminated or ignored, primarily because it did not serve directly the interests of colonizers and later of capitalists. This elimination process was particularly drastic in those regions that had achieved considerable progress independently of the West (for example, the Andean world), and its social consequences, such as the drop in population in Latin America that followed the Spanish conquest, were disastrous.[14] Nevertheless, some of these traditional activities remained at the periphery of economic life, to the extent that they supplied in part the means of subsistence to those involved in the productive activities that were implanted.

The demise and substitution of traditional productive activities implied a reduction in the variety of indigenous technological responses developed through time, and led to the total disappearance of many of them. Since in these regions the European counterpoint between traditional techniques and those related to scientific knowledge did not take place, but rather the new techniques were implanted once they were highly perfected, the disappearance of traditional techniques took a more radical character than in Europe. The shift from what Mumford called the polytechnic age to the monotechnic age was particularly violent in those countries with an exogenous scientific-technological base.

These three components--the scientific activity generating knowledge, the technological capabilities associated with implanted productive activities, and the traditional or indigenous technological capacity--have had practically no interactions among themselves in the countries with an exogenous scientific and technological base. Their evolution (involution in the case of the traditional technological capabilities) has taken place in isolation, and the fusion of science and production, which characterized the countries with an endogenous scientific and technological base in the West, did not occur. Moreover, the elimination of traditional technological capabilities was more traumatic and disruptive in the countries with an exogenous scientific and technological base than in those with an endogenous base.

TOWARD A STRATEGY FOR SCIENTIFIC AND TECHNOLOGICAL DEVELOPMENT

Accepting as a working hypothesis that the division between developed and underdeveloped countries corresponds to the proposed differentiation between countries with an endogenous scientific-technological base and those with an exogenous scientific-technological base, one of the key problems in the design of an autonomous development strategy becomes the method of relating in an organic fashion the conduct of scientific activities with the technological capabilities associated with both modern and traditional productive activities.

Linking Scientific Activity to Technology

From this point of view a country will achieve a level of self-reliant or autonomous development (which should not be confused with autarchic development)[15] to the extent that it acquires and expands its own scientific and technological base--that is, the degree to which it endogenizes the process of generating production technologies related to scientific discoveries. It should be noted that the problem is not one of reproducing in a mimetic way the experiences of the countries that have an endogenous scientific-technological base at present. This is neither possible nor desirable, because to tread the same path followed by these countries would lead to the same problems they are now experiencing, and would show an inability to learn from history. On the contrary, it will be necessary to endogenize the scientific-technological revolution in a selective and gradual way, choosing consciously those areas and fields of activity in which the process can succeed and grow roots.

At the same time, and in contrast to what has happened in the countries that now have an endogenous scientific and technological base, the indigenous technological tradition should not be discarded. This tradition, which usually remains diminished and lethargic (when it has avoided extinction), should be rescued and fully integrated with the development of scientific activities and the evolution of modern productive techniques. It should be made clear that this does not imply an indiscriminate return to the technological past, nor an illusory reappraisal of all traditional productive techniques.[16]

Summarizing, it is necessary to place at the core of an autonomous development strategy the fusion of the current of activities generating knowledge, together with the evolution of technological capabilities linked to modern production, and with the discriminate and systematic rescue of the traditional technological base. These three components should be integrated around problem areas of critical importance for the country's development strategy, and should lead to the progressive substitution of the exogenous technological base, although accepting that this is a slow process viable only in the long term. The identification of an initial set and a sequence of problem areas in which this integration can be achieved thus becomes one of the main issues to be settled.

Coexistence of Modern and Traditional Technologies

In addition to linking scientific activity to the technology involved in modern production and to traditional technologies, it is necessary to create appropriate conditions for the harmonic coexistence of modern and traditional activities, and of their respective technological bases. This implies a substantial revision and reformulation of economic concepts such as obsolescence and efficiency; the experience of the People's Republic of China may prove to be valuable in this regard.[17]

Given the magnitude of the effort required to put in practice the strategy for scientific-technological development suggested in this study, it is obvious that its viability will be conditioned by the proper identification of problem areas in which the fusion of the three currents mentioned above can be accomplished. The experience of countries with an endogenous scientific-technological base is not very useful to this end--not only because of the differences in starting conditions, but also because those countries went through an erratic and slow process that involved a considerable waste of resources. At most, a study of their past experience should indicate mistakes to be avoided.

Identification of Problem Areas

As an initial approximation, five criteria are suggested for the identification of problem areas around which to center efforts. The first criterion derives from the need to secure a critical mass to undertake scientific activities, and this should be examined from the quantitative, qualitative, and interface points of view. Considering the quantitative aspect, the aim is to ensure the availability of human, physical, and financial resources above the minimum level required to generate scientific knowledge of direct interest to the problem area. From the qualitative point of view, the resources available should have the characteristics that make them suitable for the selected activity (trained and experienced scientists, equipment satisfying certain specifications, and so on). From the interface point of view, it is necessary to gather a qualitative and quantitative base of resources, not only in the scientific field of immediate interest for the problem area, but also in those neighboring fields that interact strongly with the main axis, since advances in science frequently come about from the combination of knowledge generated in adjoining fields.

The second criterion derives from the fact that identifying problem areas in which to promote the merger of scientific advances with traditional and modern technological capabilities must be country-specific, and must be done by taking into account the social and historical context, as well as the availability of natural and human resources. The identification of problem areas should also be country-specific in the sense of being closely linked to the style of development chosen and designed.

The third criterion for the identification of a problem area stems from the possible societal impact of the fusion of the three currents. The purpose is to ensure the largest possible multiplying effect of the integration of science with modern and traditional technological capabilities, both in regard to the possibility of facilitating their integration in other problem areas, and in regard to the diffusion through society of the values and points of view related to the endogenization of the scientific and technological base.

The fourth criterion to be considered should be the possibility and the opportunity of exercising world leadership, so that the country can become an internationally recognized center of scientific excellence in a particular problem area. This can be achieved through the concentration of efforts, and can eventually pave the road for a more balanced exchange of scientific knowledge and technologies with other countries.

The last criterion concerns the selection of problem areas on the basis of the possibility of obtaining concrete results in a reasonable period of time, expressed in terms of producing and utilizing technologies related to scientific findings and of linking the scientific activity with traditional technological capabilities. Moreover, the merger of the three currents in a specific problem area should serve as a starting point in undertaking the integration process in other areas, thus generating a cumulative sequence that will facilitate the growth of an endogenous scientific and technological base.

It is clear that the strategy outlined here should be complemented by the development of a capacity for regulating technology imports, primarily because it takes a long time for the endogenization process to acquire a significant magnitude. This implies the need to increase the country's bargaining power, to be informed about the scientific advances in other parts of the world and the technologies derived from them, and to improve the technology absorption capacity of the productive sector. At the same time, and given the limitations of all types faced by the underdeveloped countries, it will be also necessary to promote international collaboration agreements, particularly among underdeveloped countries with similar problem areas (see Chapter 9).[18]

CONCLUSION

The purpose of this chapter has been to contrast the situation of the countries in which productive technologies were developed on the basis of scientific discoveries with that of those where the symbiosis between science and production did not occur. This differentiation coincides with the division between developed and underdeveloped countries, and an analysis of their historical experiences leads to some reflections on possible ways in which the underdeveloped countries can internalize the processes associated with the scientific-technological revolution and its effects.

The brief analysis of the way in which scientific advances were united with the evolution of productive techniques in the West shows that this was a process long in maturing. Resource constraints and the limited room for maneuvering inherent in the condition of underdevelopment makes the internalization of the scientific-technological revolution an improbable and difficult task. However, history shows that relying on an endogenous scientific and technological base is necessary to satisfy the basic needs of the population in an autonomous way and to allow for the full development of human potentialities, whichever style or model of development is chosen. For this reason, the endogenization of the scientific-technological revolution is a task that should be initiated without delay in the underdeveloped countries, particularly in view of the slowness of the process and the difficulties involved.

NOTES

1. See James G. Frazer, The Golden Bough, ed. Theodore Gaster (New York: Mentor Books, 1964). For a slightly different interpretation of this evolution see Bronislaw Malinowski, Una teoría científica de la Cultura (Buenos Aires: Ed. Sudamérica, 1976). (Translation of "A Scientific Theory of Culture and Other Essays," first published in 1948.)

2. On these issues, see Máximo Halty, "Towards a New Technological Order?" paper presented at the OECD seminar on Science, Technology and Development in a Changing World, Paris, April 1975.

3. On these issues see Charles Singer, From Magic to Science (New York: Dover, 1958).

4. Karl Marx, Das Capital (Middlesex: Penguin Books, 1976), vol. 1, ch. 15.

5. Lewis Mumford, The Myth of the Machine (New York: Harcourt Brace, 1972), ch. 6.

6. See Alfred E. Musson, ed., Science, Technology and Economic Growth in the 18th Century (Cambridge: Cambridge University Press, 1972); David Landes, The Unbound Prometheus (Cambridge: Cambridge University Press, 1969); and John D. Bernal, Science in History (Cambridge, Mass.: MIT Press, 1971).

7. See Karl Polanyi, The Great Transformation (New York: Harper Torchbooks, 1969).

8. Mumford, op. cit.

9. Jorge Sabato, Empresas y Fábricas de Tecnología (Washington, D.C.: Department of Scientific Affairs, OAS, 1972); and David Noble, America by Design (New York: Knopf, 1977).

10. Fritz Machlup, The Production and Distribution of Knowledge in the United States (Princeton: Princeton University Press, 1962).

11. Joseph Ben-David, The Scientists' Role in Society (New Jersey: Prentice-Hall, 1972).

12. Simon Kuznets, Population, Capital and Growth (New York: Norton, 1971), pp. 165-85.

13. See S. N. Sen, "The Introduction of Western Science in India during the 18th and the 19th Century," in Science, Technology and Culture, ed. Surajit Sinha (New Delhi: India International Centre, 1970).

14. See Richard Konetzke, América Latina: La Época Colonial (Mexico: Siglo XXI, 1972), pp. 93-98.

15. On this subject, see Francisco Sagasti, Tecnología, Planificación y Desarrollo Autónomo (Lima: IEP, 1977).

16. See Amilcar Herrera, Scientific and Traditional Technologies in Developing Countries, Science Policy Research Unit, Sussex University, April 1974.

17. See Genevieve Dean, Technology and Industrialization in the People's Republic of China, Office of the Field Coordinator, STPI Project, Lima, July 1976.

18. Also see Francisco Sagasti and Mauricio Guerrero, El Desarrollo Científico y Tecnológico de América Latina (Buenos Aires: BID/INTAL, 1974), Ch. 3.

ABOUT THE AUTHOR

FRANCISCO R. SAGASTI was born in Lima, Peru. At present he is advisor to the Senior Vice-President of the International Development Research Centre (Canada) based at the Latin American Regional office in Bogotá, Colombia. During 1973-76 he was coordinator of an international research project on technological development in Third World countries, with the participation of ten countries and more than 150 researchers. Previously he served in the Department of Scientific Affairs of the Organization of American States in Washington and Lima, the Secretariat of the Andean Common Market in Lima, and the University of Pennsylvania in Philadelphia. He obtained his Ph.D. at the University of Pennsylvania, his M.Sc. at Pennsylvania State University, and two engineering degrees at the National University in Lima, Peru. He has served as a consultant in Lima, London, Washington, Philadelphia, and other cities. He was also Vice-Chairman of the Board of the Industrial Technology Institute in Lima, Peru, during 1972-77. Dr. Sagasti has presided at conferences in Africa, Asia, Latin America, the Middle East, Europe, and North America; and has published more than fifty papers on science and technology policy, systems analysis, management sciences, and development strategies. He has published three books in Spanish, of which the most recent is Tecnología, Planificación y Desarrollo Autónomo (Lima: Instituto de Estudios Peruanos, 1977). He has also published two books in English, the most recent of which is Science and Technology for Development: Main Comparative Report of the STPI Project (Ottawa: International Development Research Center [IDRC], 1978).